Celtic Miracles and Wonders

Tales of the Ancient Saints

Celtic
Miracles and Wonders

Tales of the Ancient Saints

Meg Llewellyn, editor

ANAMCHARA
BOOKS

Celtic Miracles and Wonders:
Tales of the Ancient Saints

Anamchara Books
Vestal, NY 13850
www.anamcharabooks.com

Paperback ISBN: 978-1-62524-275-4

Edited by Meg Llewellyn.

Contents

Introduction

The twenty-first century is fascinated by the ancient Celts. For both Christians and Pagans, the long-ago Celts seem to offer an alternative way of looking at life, a more holistic way that perceives the sacred in the ordinary, that spiritually communes with Nature, and that consciously seeks to bless both the human and the natural worlds. We yearn for what the Celts had, and many of us seek to recreate it in our own lives.

We are not alone in this longing for all things Celtic. It's nothing new. In the 1700s, people in England became interested once again in the Druids and sought to bring druidry back to life. Later, in the nineteenth century, the poet William Butler Yeats was at the center of what is know as the Celtic Revival, a movement that sought to reaffirm a

Gaelic spiritual heritage amid the encroaching British culture.

Today, we who love the Celtic world often struggle between history and romanticism. Some us are taken to task for not being more historically accurate, for creating an imaginary Celtic world that probably never existed anywhere except within the pages of our favorite fantasy novels. Yeats and his colleagues looked at things a bit differently. Their interests lay not in history so much as in the present. They sought to discover and affirm the living Celtic spirit amid the ordinary people of their day—a still-growing and real outlook on the nature of reality.

The Celtic Revival was made up of artists, poets, playwrights, authors, and folklorists. They recognized the importance of the imagination and the arts in Celtic culture, and they sought to bring to life that creative legacy. Many of them—including Yeats—did so by talking to ordinary people, collecting their stories, and then recording them.

Two women who collected these stories into books were Lady Augusta Gregory and Ella Young.

They wrote and published books that included *Celtic Wonder Tales and Visions and Beliefs in the West of Ireland.* Meanwhile, in Scotland, folklorist Alexander Carmichael was doing something quite similar, though he focused on prayers and charms rather than stories. These authors, and others besides them, sought to preserve the flavor of the actual words spoken by ordinary people. They were scholars—but they were folklorists not historians.

Lady Gregory wrote, "To gather folk-lore one needs, I think, leisure, patience, reverence, and a good memory. I tried not to change or alter anything, but to write down the very words in which the story had been told. Sometimes Mr. Yeats was with me at the telling; or I would take him to hear for himself something I had been told, that he might be sure I had missed or added nothing. I filled many copybooks, and came to have a very faithful memory for all sides of folk-lore, stories of saints, of heroes, of giants and enchanters, as well as for these visions."

The stories contained in this book, *Celtic Miracles and Wonders,* are drawn from the work of Lady

Gregory, Ella Young, William Yeats, and others. They tell of the ancient Celtic saints—of Patrick and Brigit, Columcille and many others—in the words and sequences used by ordinary people. I have edited them a bit, to make them easier for modern readers, but I've left intact the cadence and flow, as well as the blunt and sometimes nearly comical acceptance of life's harsher realities.

There are other accounts of these saints' lives, many that are far more historically accurate, but those contained here tell us as much about the people who told the stories as they do about the ancient saints. They show us those saints' legacy lived out in people's lives and imaginations more than a thousand years later.

The power and vitality of that legacy is impressive. These stories reveal an ongoing conviction that the invisible world is as real as the visible one. They show us human beings living in constant, tangible friendship with God, with the supernatural, and with animals. We need not believe that Saint Brigit actually hung her cloak on a sunbeam or that bees created a tiny altar for saying Mass to be inspired and challenged by these stories. They lead us into a world where holiness and the imagination have joined hands, a world where we can truly catch glimpses of miracles and wonders.

Yeats wrote that "when imagination is impoverished, a principal voice—some would say the only voice—for the awakening of wise hope and durable faith, and understanding charity" is broken or falls silent. He continued:

> are there not moods which need heaven, hell, purgatory, and faeryland for their expression, no less than this dilapidated earth? Nay, are there not moods which shall find no expression unless there be men who dare to mix heaven, hell, purgatory, and faeryland together, or even to set the heads of beasts to the bodies of men, or to thrust the souls of men into the heart of rocks? Let us go forth, the tellers of tales, and seize whatever prey the heart long for, and have no fear. Everything exists, everything is true. . . .

Yeats considered William Blake, the eighteenth-century poet, to be the spiritual mentor who had led him into a new understanding of the Celtic imagination. For both Blake and Yeats, the power of the imagination is not recreational; it is a deeply spiritual faculty that empowers us to change the world—to bring about justice. It is not make-believe and fantasy but instead allows us to see a deeper truth. Both Blake and Yeats believed that Christ comes to us in the power of the imagination.

So the stories collected here can be read because they're entertaining. They *are* entertaining, and those who told them back in the nineteenth century were also entertained by them. But they are more than fun and fanciful little stories. In Yeats' words, those "who would re-awaken imaginative tradition by making old songs live again or by gathering stories into books" are taking part in the Gospel, the telling of the Good News that God lives among us and we are called to make Divine justice, generosity, and gentleness real in the world around us.

May these stories awaken us to a wiser hope, a more durable faith, and more discerning love.

—*Meg Llewellyn*

PART I

BLESSED PATRICK OF THE BELLS

When we hear the name Saint Patrick, many of us think instantly of shamrocks and leprechauns, parades and corned beef. His name has become nearly synonymous with all things Irish. But Patrick is not only a cultural symbol. He was also a real person.

Stories about Patrick abound, some historical and some embellished through the years. Many of these express spiritual truth, even if they are not factual. We know for certain that he was a fifth-century Christian missionary and bishop in Ireland. By the seventh century, he was already said to be Ireland's patron saint, and he and Saint Brigit are still considered the most important Irish saints.

Most of what we know about Patrick stems from three sources: First, are two fifth-century letters written by Patrick himself, and in one of these he gives a short account of his life and mission. His biography was next written down in the seventh century by two hagiographers, Tirechan and Muirchu. Both writers relied on an earlier work, the *Book of Ultan*, which has since been lost. Ultan is thought to have been the foster father of Tirechan, so Tirechan would have likely grown up hearing stories about Patrick.

According to his hagiographers, Patrick's original name was Maewyn Succat, a name that meant "strong in war." He later took the name Patrick, from the Latin for "father." (Tirechan mysteriously states that Patrick's Celtic name was Coithraige, "because he served four houses of druids.")

Tirechan and Muirchu portray a martial Patrick who fights with the druids and curses kings and kingdoms. Their tales don't always agree with Patrick's own account of his life, and they may instead more accurately reflect seventh-century attitudes. Both hagiographers also stress, however, what is thought to a historical aspect of Patrick's work: as many women followed him as men. He also worked with slaves and the poor, encouraging them to join one of the many monasteries he founded.

Much about Patrick remains a mystery—but a few things we do know for certain: he was a deeply spiritual man, a man of great courage, who brought a lasting change to the land he loved so much.

1
Slavery and Freedom

There were many great saints among the Gael, but Patrick was the bush among them all. It was beyond the sea he was born, and his mother was a sister of Saint Martin of Tours; and he dreamed in Rome, and walked all Ireland barefoot. In his young youth he was brought from France to Ireland as a slave, and he was set to serve four households, and he did his work so well that every one of the households thought him to be its servant alone. But it was an angel who helped him do so much work.

He was sent out after a while minding swine and he went through great hardships; but Victor the angel used to come to visit him and to teach him the order of prayer. And he had no way to buy his freedom, but one time a wild boar came rooting in the field, and brought up a lump of gold; and Patrick brought it to a tinker and the tinker said, "It is nothing but solder, give it here to me."

But then he brought it to a smith, and the smith told him it was gold and with that gold he brought his freedom. And from that time the smiths have been lucky, taking money every day and never without work.

The Man and Woman Who Were Always Young

After that he went out to sea with foreigners and he went back to his own country, and his people asked him to stop there with them. But he would not, for always in his sleep he could see the island of the Gael, and he could hear the singing of the children of the Wood of Fochlad. He went over the sea of Icht then, and he fasted in the islands of the Torrian Sea, and then he went to learn from Germanus, and after that again to Rome. And then he and his people went out to sea, nine in all, and they came to an island where they saw a new house, and a young man and a young woman in it, with a withered old hag by the door of the house.

"What happened to this old woman?" said Patrick. "Why is she so weak?"

"She is my own grandchild, old as she is," said the young man.

"How did that happen?" said Patrick.

"It is not hard to explain," said the young man. "For we are here from the time of Christ," he said, "and He came to visit us when He was here among men, and we made a feast for Him and He blessed our house and He blessed our bodies, but the blessing did not reach to our children. And this is the way we will be, without age coming upon us, until the end of time. Your coming was foretold to us long ago," he said, "and it is the will of God for you to go and to preach in the country of the Gael. Christ left a token with us, a bent staff to be given to you."

2
Patrick Goes Back to Ireland

Patrick took the staff with him then and went back to Germanus. And Victor the angel came in a vision to him, carrying many letters. He gave one of the letters to Patrick, and he saw that it was titled "The Voice of the Irish." As he began to read, he heard a great number of people crying out with one voice, "We appeal to you, holy servant boy, to come and walk among us."

But Patrick was not willing to go and he complained to God of the hardheartedness of the Gael.

And God said, "I myself will be your helper."

Then Patrick went back to Rome and he was made a bishop. While they were making a bishop of him. three quires sang: the quire of the people of

Heaven, the quire of the Romans, and the quire of the children faraway in the Wood of Fochlad in the east of Ireland where he landed, at Inis Patrick.

In Ireland, meanwhile the druids had foretold his coming: "Adzeheads will come over an angry sea; their cloaks hole-headed; their staves crooked; their tables to the east of their houses; they will all say, 'so be it, so be it,' again and again."

At the time Patrick landed it was the feast of Beltaine, and on that day every year the High King lighted a fire in Teamhuir. And on that day, it was forbidden that anyone kindle a fire anywhere else besides the fire in Teamhuir. Patrick, now, struck the flame of the Paschal fire, and all the people saw it. It lighted up the whole of Magh Breg.

"That is a breaking of bonds," said the king to his druids. "Find out for me," he said, "who was it kindled that fire."

And the druids said, "Unless that fire is quenched before morning in the same night it was kindled, it will never be quenched."

And the druids spoke true, for Patrick's fire still burns in the light of Heaven.

The Deer's Cry

One time as Patrick and Benen were going to preach the Faith at Teamhuir, his enemies lay in hiding to make an attack on him as he passed. But Patrick sang a hymn, and as he and Benen went by, all that could be seen passing were a wild deer and a fawn. And the Deer's Cry is the name of the hymn to this day.

I bind myself today to a strong strength,
to a calling on the Trinity.
I believe in a Threeness
with confession of a Oneness
in the Creator of the World.

I bind myself today
to the strength of Christ's birth and his baptism;
to the strength of his crucifixion with his burial;
to the strength of his resurrection with his ascension.

In stability of earth,
in steadfastness of rock,

I bind to myself today God's strength
to pilot me;
God's power to uphold me;
God's wisdom to guide me;
God's eye to look before me;
God's ear to hear me;
God's word to speak for me;
God's hand to guard me;
God's path to lie before me;
God's shield to protect me;
God's host to save me;
against snares of demons;
against the begging of sins;
against the asking of nature;
against all my ill-wishers
near me and far from me;
alone and in a crowd.

So I have called on all these strengths,
to come between me
and every fierce and merciless strength
that may come between my body and my soul;

Christ for my protection
against poison, against burning,
against drowning, against wounding,
against ill-speaking.

Christ with me, Christ before me;
Christ behind me, Christ in me;
Christ under me, Christ over me;
Christ to the right of me, Christ to the left of me;
Christ in lying down, Christ in sitting,
Christ in rising up;
Christ in the heart of everyone that thinks of me;
Christ in the mouth of everyone that speaks to me;
Christ in every eye that sees me;
Christ in every ear that hears me.

I bind to myself today a strong strength
to a calling upon the Trinity;
I believe in a Threeness
with confession of a Oneness
in the Creator of the World!

3
Patrick and the Big Men from Out of the Past

Patrick was one time singing the Mass at the Rath of the Red Ridge where Finn, son of Cumhal, used to be long ago. And Patrick's clerks saw Caoilte and his people coming toward them, and fear and terror fell on them, for the clerks knew these great men came from another time, and they and their hounds were greater than any man or hound then living.

But Patrick, the high herdsman, angel of the earth, simply stood up and sprinkled holy water upon the big men, and with that, any bad thing that lingered about them made away into the hills and the borders of the country on every side. The big men sat down with Patrick and his clerks. The clerks were filled with wonder as they looked at them, for the tallest of the clerks reached but to the waist or shoulders of the great men—and they were sitting.

"What name have you?" said Patrick then.

"I am Caoilte, son of Ronan of the Fianna."

"Was it not the good lord you were with," said Patrick, "that is Finn, son of Cumhal?"

And Caoilte said, "If the brown leaves falling in the woods were gold, if the waves of the sea were silver, Finn would have given away the whole of it, so generous was he."

"What was it kept you through your lifetime?" said Patrick.

"Truth that was in our hearts, and strength in our hands, and fulfilment in our tongues," said Caoilte.

Then Patrick gave them food and drink and good treatment and talked with them. And on the morning of the morrow, his two protecting angels came to him out of the green, and Patrick asked them was it any harm before the King of Heaven and earth, for him to be listening to the stories of the Fianna.

And the angels answered him: "Holy Clerk," they said, "it is no more than a third of their stories these old fighting-men can tell, by reason of forgetfulness and their memory that fails them; but whatever they tell, write it down on poets' boards and in the words of poets, for it will be well for the people of the latter times to be listening to them."

And Patrick did as they bade him, and he bade Brogan the scribe to write down all the stories told by Caoilte; and Brogan did that, and they are in the world to this day.

The Hidden Well of Usnach

One time Diarmuid king of Ireland was with Patrick on the Hill of Usnach, and there was no water to be had. One of the big men of the Fianna—it might have been Caoilte and it might have been Oisin—asked for a vessel that he might go and get it. And as he went, he was looking back to see if they were watching him. When he was out of their sight, he went to the Well of Usnach, the White-Brimmed Well, and since the time of the battle of Gabra it had never been found by any person in Ireland.

And when he came to the brink of the well, he saw in it eight beautiful speckled salmon, for it was such a hidden place there was nothing for them to dread. He took then eight sprigs of watercress and eight of brooklime, and he put down the vessel into the well and he took the eight salmon alive and leaping like mad things. And then he went back and set the vessel before the King of Ireland, and there was wonder on them all seeing that. The stalk of every one of the sprigs of the watercress reached as high as Diarmuid's knee.

"They must be divided into two shares," he said, "a half for Patrick and a half for ourselves."

"Not so," said Patrick, "for there are more of you than of ourselves. But make three parts," he said, "and give one to the church for that is her own share." And so it was done.

"That is well, King of Ireland," he said then, "but do not lose your share in heaven through these big men."

"What do you mean saying that?" said Diarmuid.

"I mean that you have your thoughts too much taken up with them," said Patrick. "They stand between your eyes and the Heaven that is all around you."

Patrick and Cascorach the Musician

One time the King of Ulster went up with Caoilte to a place called Foradh-na-Feinne, the Resting-Place of the Fianna. And when they were there, they saw coming towards them a young man wearing a beautiful green cloak having on it a silver brooch; a shirt of yellow silk he wore next to his skin; a coat of soft satin he wore, and a harp hung from his neck.

"Where do you come from and who are you yourself?" said the King.

"I come from the South from the Hill of Bodb Dearg son of the Dagda," said he, "and I am Cascorach, son of Cainchen that is poet to the Tuatha de Danaan and I am the makings of a poet myself. And it is what I am come for now," he said, "to get true knowledge and the stories of the Fianna and their great deeds from Caoilte son of Ronan."

With that he took his harp and made music for them till he had put them all asleep.

"Well, Caoilte, my soul," he said then, "what answer will you give me?"

"I will give you all you are asking," said Caoilte, "if you have skill and understanding to learn all the Fianna did of arms and of bravery. And it was a great fighting-man used to be in this place," he said, "that was Finn, son of Cumhal, and it is great riches and great wages you would have got from him for your music; although this day the place is empty."

And he made this lament:

The Resting-place of the Fianna is bare tonight
where Finn of the naked sword used to be;
through the death of the king
that was without gloom,
wide Almhuin is deserted.

The high company are not living;
Finn the very prince is not alive;
no armies to be seen,
no captains with the King of the Fianna.

They are all gone, the people of Finn,
they that used to be going from valley to valley;
it is a pity the life I have now,

to be left after Diarmwd and Conan,
after Goll son of Morna from the plain.

It is the truth I am telling you;
all that I say is true;
it is great our losses were there beyond.
They are gone, the armies and the hundreds;
it is a pity I myself not to have found death;
they are all gone now;
they used to be together from border to border.

Then Caoilte brought to mind the loss of the heroes and his old companions of long ago, and he cried miserably, sorrowfully, till all his breast was wet. He set out after that and Cascorach with him, and they went up by hills and rocks to the top of green-grassed Slieve Fuad, to the rowan tree of the Meadow of the Two Stags and to the place where the men of Ulster left their chariots after the last battle of the War for the Bull of Cuailgne.

And Patrick was there before him, having with him three times fifty bishops and three times fifty priests and three times fifty deacons and three times fifty singers of psalms. And they sat down there, and Patrick kept his Hours with praising the Maker of the world. Then he gave a welcome to Caoilte.

"Well, my soul," he said, "who is that well-looking dark-eyebrowed curly-headed young man that is with you, having a harp with him?"

"He is Cascorach son of the musician of the Tuatha De Danaan, that is come to find news and knowledge of the Fianna from me."

"It is a good road he has chosen," said Patrick. "And O Caoilte," he said, "it is great good you yourself have waited for, the time of belief and of saints and of holiness, and to be in friendship with the King of Heaven and earth. And play to us now Cascorach," he said, "till we hear your music and your skill."

"I will do that," said Cascorach, "and I never was better pleased, holy Clerk, to do it for any soul than for yourself."

He took his harp then and readied it, and played a strain of music, and the clerks had never heard the like of that music for sweetness, unless it might be the praises of the King of Heaven sung according to the Rule. And they all fell asleep listening to the music of the Sidhe. And when Cascorach had made an end of playing, he asked a reward of Patrick.

"What reward are you asking, my soul?" said Patrick.

"Heaven for myself," said he, "for that is the best reward; and good luck to go with my art and with all that will follow it after me."

"I give you Heaven," said Patrick, "and I give this to your art, that it will be one of the three arts by which the people in Ireland can find profit forever. And that they may have all happiness," he said, "so long as they are not slothful in their trade."

After that Cascorach put back his harp in its covering."

"That was good music you gave us," said Brogan the scribe.

"It was good indeed," said Patrick, "and though it had a taste of the music of the Sidhe in it, I never heard anything nearer to the music of Heaven."

"If there is music in Heaven, why should it not be on earth?" said Brogan. "And so it is not right to banish it away."

"I do not say we should banish it," said Patrick, "but only that we should listen to it in measure, as in all things."

Patrick's Farewell to Caoilte

After a good while, Caoilte said at last, "Holy Patrick, my soul, I am thinking it is time for me to be going tomorrow."

"Why would you go?" said Patrick.

"To be searching out the hills and the hollows of every place where my comrades and the King of the Fianna used to be together with me, for it seems long to me to be in one place."

And when they rose up on the morrow, Caoilte laid his hand in Patrick's bosom, and Patrick said, "From myself to yourself, in the house or out of the house, in whatever place God will lay His hand on you, I give you Heaven."

4
Patrick's Work

Once, in obedience to his angel Victor, Patrick went into the hills for forty days alone, and there he prayed without stopping for Ireland. The demons that made Ireland their battlefield did their best to disturb his solitude and turn him away from his prayers. When he looked out from the hill where he sat, he saw a vast flock of hideous birds of prey gathered around the hill on all sides, like a dark cloud. Patrick asked God to scatter the demons, but the birds seemed to grow in number, until they came between him and the sky and the sun. At length, he rang his bell. Its sweetness sang over all Ireland, over the valleys and hills, everywhere bringing peace and joy. The black flocks scattered. Then Patrick drew back his arm and flung his bell among the birds. They took flight in a rush, and cast themselves into the ocean. So complete was Patrick's victory over evil, that for seven years no evil could be found in Ireland

Patrick used to give out bells to the people wherever he went, and the bells were to them like the voice of God. These bells were rung in times of storm and danger, as well as to call the people to their prayers. The bells rang out at each turn of life, speaking of the God of Heaven and His ever-love. When a soul came to its last hour, when nothing remained but weariness, the bell sounded then like the voice of an old friend, strengthening the soul with hope. And when the soul was gone, the ringing of the bell reminded those who still lived to help those who are dead with prayers.

And Patrick is the one who first brought the bells to Ireland. He carried with him always a bell.

Bodb Dearg's Daughter

Aedh King of Connacht was at Dun Leoda Loingsig one time giving a great feast. At the fall of the clouds of evening, he came out on the green lawn, and as he was there and the people of his household with him, he saw on one side a girl of wonderful appearance, having yellow hair. She was not looking at the people but only at the King.

"Where do you come from, girl?" said the King.

"Out of the shining Brugh in the east," said she.

"For what cause are you come?" said the King.

"You are my sweetheart," said she.

"Whose daughter are you and what name have you?" said the King.

"I am Aillenn of the many shapes, daughter to Bodb Dearg, son of the Dagda."

"I have never seen a woman I would sooner have as a wife than yourself," said the King, "but I am under the rule of Blessed Patrick and of the King of Heaven and earth. And Patrick bound me," he said, "to have one wife only, that is Aife daughter of Eoghan, King of Leinster. But will you not show yourself now to the people of my kingdom?" he said.

"I will indeed," said she, "for I am not an ever-living woman of the Sidhe, but I am of the Tuatha de Danaan, having my own body about me." Then she showed herself to the whole gathering of the people, and they never saw before or after a woman more beautiful than herself.

"And what judgment do you put upon me, King?" she said.

"Whatever judgment Blessed Patrick gives, I will give it," said he.

Then Aedh sent messengers to Patrick where he was in the south, and they brought him to Beinn Gulbain in Maenmag. And Aedh the King went to meet him there and knelt before him and told him the whole story.

"Are you the girl," said Patrick to her, "that gave her love to the King of Connacht?"

"I am," said she.

"Well, girl," said Patrick, "your shape is lovely and your appearance good. What is it that keeps you like this," he said, "at the very height of your comeliness?"

"Everyone that drank at Giobniu's Feast," she said, "no sickness or wasting comes upon them. And tell me now, holy Clerk," she said, "what is your judgment on myself and on the King of Connacht?"

"It is a good one," said Patrick. "It is settled by God and myself that a man must have one wife only."

"But what about myself?" said the girl. "What am I to do?"

"Go back to your house among the Sidhe," said Patrick, "and if it should happen the King of Leinster's daughter die before yourself, let the man you have given your love to take you as his only wife. But if you should try to harm Aedh or his wife by day or by night," he said, "I will destroy you."

Then the girl cried pitifully, heavily, and the King said, "I am dear to you."

"You are dear to me indeed," said she.

"There is no one now dearer to me than yourself," said the King, "but I must not go beyond the conditions of the Adzehead and of God."

With that, the girl went back to her hidden house among the Sidhe. And after a while the wife of the King of Connacht died at Uaran Garaid and was buried on the hill that is called the High Place of the Angels. And after that again there was a gathering made of all the five provinces of Ireland to hold the feast of Teamhuir. And Patrick and Aedh King of Connacht were out on the green, when they saw coming toward them Aillenn daughter of Bodb Dearg, having with her three fifties of the women of the Tuatha de Danaan. She sat down on the grass beside Patrick and the King of Connacht, and she gave her message.

Then Patrick said to the King, "I will give her to you if you will take her as your wife."

"Whatever you are willing for me to do, I will do it," said the King."

"I promised you would take her," said Patrick.

Then she rose up, and her women with her, and they all kneeled to Patrick, and Patrick joined her and the King in marriage. That was the first marriage made by the Adzehead in Ireland.

The Soul and the Body

The Savior told Patrick one time to go and prepare a man who was going to die. But Patrick said, "I would sooner not go for I never yet saw the soul part from the body."

But he went anyway and prepared the man for his death. And when the man was lying there dead, Patrick saw the soul go from the body. Three times the soul went to the door and three times it came back and kissed the body.

Patrick asked the Savior, "Why is the soul doing that?"

He said, "That soul is sorry to part from the body for it served him well. He loves it and he is loath to leave it behind."

Ethne the Beautiful and Fedeim the Rosy-Red

Patrick was one time at Cruachan of Connacht, and he went up to the well that is called Clibach that is opposite the rising of the sun. He sat down beside the well, and his clerks with him. There were two daughters now of Laoghaire the High King who were living at Rath Cruachan at that time, getting their learning from the druids, and the name of the one was Ethne and the other was Fedeim the Rosy-Red.

And it was their custom every morning to come and to wash themselves in the well.

And on this day when they came, they saw a company of men in white clothes beside the well, their books before them. Ethne and Fedeim were filled with wonder, for they thought them to be of the people of the Sidhe. And they questioned Patrick and said to him, "Where do you come from? And where are you going? And is it gods you are," they said, "or men from the hills of the Sidhe?"

"It matters little who we are," said Patrick. "It would be better for you to believe in God than worry who we are."

"Who is your God?" said Ethne then. "And where is He?" she said. "Is He in the skies is, or in the earth, or under the earth, or upon the earth, or in the seas or in the streams, or in the mountains or in the valleys? And has He riches?" she said. "Is He young? Is He beautiful? Has He sons and daughters? Is He of the ever-living ones?"

Patrick took in hand then to tell them of the Trinity and the story of Christ, Prince of Heaven and earth. "The Son is one with God," said Patrick.

"The Son is not younger than the Father. The Father is not older than the Son. And the Holy Ghost proceeds from them both the same. They are One Being in love," he said, "and we are loved like a bride is loved."

And when the two women had heard the whole story, a great yearning came upon them to serve the Trinity.

"Our hearts' desire," they said, "is to see now the Son, our Husband. Will you show Him to us?"

"That is not possible," said Patrick, "except through taking the body of Christ and through death."

"Then we will die," they said, "if that means we will see Christ at the next moment."

Then Patrick baptized them and gave them the Body of Christ. They put white veils upon their heads, and they were filled with peace and with the friendship of God.

And when they were sleeping in death, his people put them in a little grave and laid coverings over them, and keened them there.

Patrick's Rush Candles

Patrick went one time into a poor house in the south. The people who lived there had not a candle or a rush light or turf or sticks for a fire. When the daylight was done, they had to go to bed for they had no light.

When Patrick came in and saw the house so dark, he said, "Are there no green rushes growing in the bog?"

So they went out and brought him in a bundle of green rushes. He took them in his hand and blessed them, and they gave out light through the whole of the nighttime.

His Church at Ardmacha

Patrick was walking up the hill of Ardmacha one time with his people, when they found a doe resting on the ground, and a fawn beside her. His people were going to kill the fawn, but Patrick forbade them and he took it in his arms and carried it, and the doe came following after him. And in the place where he put down the fawn, the church of Ardmacha was built for him afterwards.

Patrick and a Druid

A druid named Daire came to pay his respects to Patrick, bringing with him a wondrous cauldron of bronze. Said Daire to Patrick, "May this bronze vessel be yours."

"We give you thanks," said Patrick.

On his way home, Daire said to his servants, "Only a stupid man would say nothing but 'we give you thanks' when given such a wondrous bronze vessel. Go," he said to his servants, "and take back the cauldron and bring it back to me."

So his servants went to Patrick and said, "We have come to take back the cauldron."

"We give you thinks," said Patrick.

"What did the Christian say when you took back the vessel?" asked Daire of his servants when they returned.

"He said, 'We give you thanks,'" they told him.

"He gives thanks when he is given a gift," said Daire, "and he gives thanks when it is taken away. And I see now such statements are indeed useful to the heart. By virtue of his thankfulness, I will give back to him the bronze vessel."

Daire himself carried the cauldron back to Patrick, saying, "Here is your cauldron. You are a consistent and imperturbable man. And so I will give you not only this bronze vessel, but also a portion of my land, as much as you want, that you may feel free to dwell here."

He Is Waked by the Angels

When the time came for Patrick to die, he desired to go to Ardmacha. But Victor the angel went to meet him on the road at midday and said, "Go back to the place you came from, to the barn, for it is there your death will be. And give thanks to Christ," he said, "for your prayers are granted. You will be going soon to Heaven. You have been asleep all your life, but now the angels will wake you from the sleep that is all you have ever known."

When his soul parted from his body, there was no candle wasted on him, for the angels of God kept lasting watch over him until the end of twelve nights, and through all that time there was no night in the place because of the light of the angels. It was a long day of peace!

After his death, the men of Ulster and the Ua Neil fought for his body, and there was nearly a great battle. But at the last it seemed to them that his body was brought by each of them to his own country, and God made everyone content.

And now, the sound of Patrick's own bell is still heard at times, ringing out in hills and wood, though none sees it.

PART II

BRIGIT
THE MARY
OF THE GAEL

Like Patrick, Brigit is a historical person. She was born in the middle of the fifth century, on the threshold between Pagan Ireland and Christian Ireland, and died in the first half of the sixth century. She was a contemporary of Saint Patrick, and according to some accounts, Patrick was the bishop of the North, while she was the bishop of the South. At the very least, she was the leader of a religious community at Kildare, a well-known, well-respected, and much loved woman whose reputation eventually spread far beyond Ireland.

Symbolically, she served (and continues to serve) as a bridge between Paganism and Christianity. During her lifetime, perhaps intentionally, she took on many of the characteristics of the Goddess Brigit, who was an important and beloved member of the Celtic pantheon. Over the centuries, the saint's and the goddess's lives and stories merged, until it is difficult to distinguish one from the other.

Much like the Virgin of Guadalupe in the Americas, Brigit fostered the Christian conversion of an entire cultural group, while allowing them to maintain their own unique identity and heritage.

What we know about Brigit's life comes to us from her hagiographers, the first of which, Broccan, was born in the sixth century, when people would have still been alive who remembered her. Other hagiographies were written in the seventh century, but at the same time, stories of this beloved saint would have been handed down orally through the generations. There are many stories told about Brigit, with many variations to each story.

These tales may seem too fantastic to be factual, and yet they bring Brigit clearly to life. Nearly fifteen centuries later, she still shines as brightly, a strong, kind, and generous woman whose fiery spirit lives on, not only in Ireland, but around the world.

1
Brigit of the Sunrise

Now as to Brigit, she was born on a threshold, at sunrise on the first day of the spring, of a bondwoman of Connacht. And it was angels who baptized her and that gave her the name of Brigit, which means a Fiery Arrow.

Now Brigit's mother was not married, though she had born a child, and so she sought to hide her babe. But the newborn child was discovered by her kinsmen, and they set her adrift on the sea in a coracle. The waves and the wind carried her to a holy island, where the Druids raised her.

All the food she ate in her childhood was the milk of a white red-eared cow that had been set apart for her by one of the Druids. When she grew older, the Druids taught her all the lore of beasts and herbs and the seasons. Beloved she was by all, and like the Christ Child, she grew in wisdom, and like a little child she led them.

Brigit and the Son of Mary

When Brigit was born, her mother said it was showed to her at that time, "This child will be the Mother of God." And it came to pass like this.

The girl grew up with the Druids in that ancient place, and one day she was sitting at the door, and our Savior sent a Bright One to her who said, "Would you wish to be the Mother of God?"

"I would wish it," said she.

And on the minute, as she said that, the Savior went into her as a child. The Messenger took her with him then, and he put beautiful clothing on her, and she became so beautiful that all the people followed them, crowding to see the two beautiful people who were passing by.

They met then with Mary, the Mother of God, and Mary said to Brigit, "What can we do to make these crowds leave following us?"

"I will do that for you," said Brigit, "for I will show them a wonder."

She went into a house then and brought out a harrow and held it up over her head, and every one of the pins gave out a flame like a candle; and all the people turned back to look at the shining harrow that was such a great wonder. And it is because of this that the harrow is blessed since that time. It breaks the earth with holiness.

The Mother of God asked Brigit then what she could do for her as a reward, and Brigit laughed aloud and said, "Put my day before your own day."

So Mary did that, and Saint Brigit's Day is kept before Mary's Day ever since.

Midwife to Mary

On another night, the same Bright One came to Brigit and said, "Would you wish to see the night when our Savior was born?"

"I would wish it," said Brigit.

And so the Bright One took her to Bethlehem, and it was Mary's time. Brigit was the midwife who served Mary, and Brigit's cloak was the first to wrap around the Child. And then, when Mary fell into a sleep, so spent was she from the labor, Brigit nursed the Baby at her own breast, which suddenly flowed with milk, though she were a maiden.

And there are some say Brigit fostered the Holy Child on the journey to Egypt, and later, she kept an account of every drop of blood He lost throughout His lifetime. Anyway, we know she was always going about with the Mother of God.

2
Brigit of Great Plenty

Everything Brigit put her hand to used to increase, and it was she who wove the first piece of cloth in Ireland, long and long ago. She put the white threads in the loom that have a power of healing in them to this day. She bettered the sheep, and she satisfied the birds, and she fed the poor.

When sent to collect milk or butter as a child, she gave it all away. When a stranger asked her for a drink of water, it changed to milk, and once she gave out a barrel of beer that satisfied an entire village and more. They do also say she changed her bath-water into beer to quench the thirst of a visitor who came when not expected.

Brigit in Her Father's House

When she grew to be strong and to have good courage, she left the Druids and went to her father

Dubthach's house in Munster and stopped with him there for a while.

Once some high person came to the house, and food was made ready for him and for his people. Brigit, working in the kitchen, was given five pieces of bacon to boil for the guests. But just at that moment, there came into the kitchen a very hungry miserable hound, and she was moved with compassion by his sadness and hunger. She gave him a piece of the bacon, and when the hound was not satisfied with that, she gave him still another piece.

Then Dubthach came and asked Brigit if the five pieces of bacon were ready and none missing. "Count them then," she said to him, and he counted them. The five pieces were there, not one of them missing.

But the high guest had been sitting there all the while, though Brigit had thought him to be asleep, and he had seen all. He told her father all that happened. Then he and the people who were with him did not eat that meat, saying it was what had been given to the hound, but in truth they were not worthy of it. Brigit was happy to give it instead to the poor and the wretched.

She Minds the Dairy

After that Brigit went to visit her mother that was in bondage to a Druid of Connacht. Her mother was at that time at a grass-farm of the mountains having on it twelve cows, and she gathering butter. But there was sickness on her, and Brigit cared for her mother and took charge of the whole place. And the churning she made, she used to divide it first into twelve parts in honor of the twelve apostles of our Lord; and the thirteenth part she would make bigger than the rest, to the honor of Christ, and that part she would give to strangers and to the poor. And the serving boy wondered to see her doing that, but she said to him, "It is in the name of Christ I feed the poor; for Christ is in the body of every poor creature."

She Fills the Vessels

One time the serving boy went to the Druid's house, and he asked the boy if the girl minding the dairy was doing her job well. And the boy said, "I am thankful, and the calves are fat," for he did not want to say anything against the girl.

But the Druid got word that she was giving away the churning, and he came to visit the farm, and his wife along with him. The cows were doing well, and the calves were fat. Then they went into the dairy, having with them a vessel eighteen hands in height. And Brigit bade them welcome and washed their feet, and made ready food for them, and after that, they bade her fill up the vessel with butter.

She had but a churning and a half for them, and she went into the kitchen where it was stored and said aloud:

O my High Prince, who can do all these things,
bless my kitchen with thy right hand!
My kitchen, the kitchen of the bright Lord;
a kitchen that was blessed by my King;
a kitchen where there is butter.
My Friend is coming, the Son of Mary;
it is He blessed my kitchen;
the Prince of the world comes to this place;
that there may be plenty with Him!

After she had made that hymn, she brought the half of the churning from the place where it was stored; and the Druid's wife mocked at her and said, "I shall be glad to see how you think to fill such a large vessel with such a small churning!"

"Fill your vessel," said Brigit, "and God will add something to it." And she was going back to her kitchen and bringing half a churning every time and praying aloud every time.

And if all the vessels of the men of Munster had been brought to her she would have filled the whole of them.

The Lake of Milk

The Seven Bishops came to her in a place she had in the north Kildare, and she asked her cook had she any food to feed them, and the cook said she had not. And Brigit was ashamed, being as she was without food before those holy men, and she prayed hard to the Lord. Then angels came and bade her to milk the cows for the third time that day. So she milked them herself, and they filled the pails with the milk, and they would have filled all the vessels of the whole of Leinster. And the milk overflowed the vessels till it made a lake that is called the Lake of Milk to this day.

The Things Brigit Wished For

These were the wishes of Brigit:

I would wish a great lake of ale for the King of Kings;
I would wish the family of Heaven
to be drinking it through life and time.

I would wish the men of Heaven in my own house;
I would wish vessels of peace to be giving to them.

I would wish vessels full of alms to be giving away;
I would wish ditches of mercy for peace-making.

I would wish joy to be in their drinking;
I would wish Jesus to be here among them.

I would wish the three Mary's of great name;
I would wish the people of Heaven from every side.

I would wish to be a rent-payer to the Prince;
that way if I was in trouble
He would give me a good blessing.

Whatever, now, Brigit would ask of the Lord, He would give it to her on the moment. Each thing she touched multiplied, not for her own satisfaction but that she might satisfy each person and beast she met.

3
Kind Brigit
of Great Wisdom

And this is what her desire ever was: to satisfy the poor, to banish every hardship, and to save every sorrowful person.

The Man That Had Lost His Wife's Love

Brigit would give herself to no man in marriage but she did great wonders and blessed others. There came to her one time a man making his complaint that his wife would not sleep with him but was leaving him, and he came asking a spell from Brigit that would bring back her love.

And Brigit blessed water for him, and said: "Bring that water into your house, and put it in the food and in the drink and on the bed."

And after he had done that, his wife gave him great love, so that she could not be as far as the other side of the house from him, but was always at his hand.

And one day he set out on a journey, leaving the wife in her sleep, and as soon as she awoke from her sleep she rose up and followed after her man till she saw him. There was a strip of the sea between them, and she called out to him, that if he would not come back to her, she would go into the sea that was between them.

So much did the wife love and long for her husband after Brigit blessed the marriage.

The Drying of Brigit's Cloak

One time Brennain, saint of the Gael, came from the west to Brigit, to the Plain of the Life, for he wondered at the great name she had for doing miracles and wonders. And Brigit came in from her sheep to welcome him, and as she came into the house, she hung her cloak that was wet on the rays of the sun, and they held it up the same as hooks.

The King of Leinster's Fox

One time there was a man of her household cutting firewood, and he chanced to kill a pet fox belonging to the King of Leinster. The King's sadness made him cruel, and he had the man made prisoner.

But Brigit called a fox out of the wood, and he came and was at his tricks and his games for the King and his people at Brigit's bidding. Thus was the King made happy again. And when the fox had done his tricks, he went away safe through the wood, and the army of Leinster, footmen and horsemen and hounds, after him, but they could not catch him.

Brigit and the Boar

Another time, hunters were after a boar, and they chased the beast onto Brigit's land at Kildare. They thought to kill it there, but Brigit barred their way, and she said, "This is place of sanctuary. You cannot kill this boar on holy ground."

The hunters argued with her, saying that this was a rule for persons and not beasts, but Brigit prevailed. The boar was not killed, and the hunters went on their way.

Then she laid her hands on the beast and prayed, and he became as sweet natured as any dog. For the rest of his days, he was following at Brigit's footsteps as she went about her work.

Brigit Spreads Her Cloak

When she was a poor girl, she was minding her cow one time at the Curragh of Life, and she had no place to feed it but the side of the road. And a rich man that owned the land came by and saw her and said, "How much land would it take to give grass to the cow?"

"As much as my cloak would cover," said she.

"I will give you that," said the rich man.

She laid down her cloak then, and it was spreading out miles and miles on every side.

But there was a silly old woman passing by and she said, "If that cloak goes on spreading, all Ireland will no more be free," and with that the cloak stopped and spread no more. And Brigit held that land through her lifetime, and it never had rent on it since, but the English Government have taken it now and have put barracks upon it. It is a pity the old woman spoke that line. She did not know Brigit to be better than other ones are.

The Leper Who Would Be a King

A leper came one time to Brigit, asking a cow. And Brigit said, "Would you sooner have a cow or be healed of your disease?"

"I would sooner be healed," he said, "than to have the sway over the whole world. For every sound man is a king," he said.

Then Brigit prayed to God; and the leper was healed, and served her afterwards.

Brigit Helps a Woman

A woman who had taken a vow of virginity had weakened and forsaken her vow. When her belly swelled, she came to Brigit and asked her if she would but bless her. Brigit called on Mary's Son to bless the woman, and that which had been conceived in her womb grew no more but disappeared. The woman was healed without any pain of childbirth.

The Son of Reading

One time she was minding her sheep on the Curragh, and she saw a son of Reading running past her.

"What is it makes you so uneasy," she said, "and what is it you are looking for?"

"It is to Heaven I am running, woman," said the scholar.

"The Virgin's Son knows whoever makes that journey is happy," said Brigit. "I ask you, pray to God to make it easy for myself to go there."

"I have no time," said he, "for the gates of Heaven are open now, and I am in dread they might be shut against me."

"How can Heaven shut its door on one who stops to help another?" asked she.

"Well and well," he said then, "as you are hindering me, pray to the Master to make it easy for me to go there, and I will pray Him to make it easy for you."

Then they took hands in friendship, and he tarried after all. They sat down and said "Our Father," together, and he was not the same after. He became a holy brother and it was he who gave her absolution at the last.

And it is by reason of him that the whole of the sons of learning of the world are with Brigit.

The Fishes Honor Her

Brennain came to Brigit one time to ask why was it the beasts of the sea gave honor to her more than to the rest of the saints. Then they made their confession to each other, and Brennain said after that, "In my opinion, girl, it is right the beasts are when they honor you above the rest of us who are men."

A Hymn Made for Brigit by Brennain or Another

Brigit, excellent woman;
sudden flame;
may the bright fiery sun
bring us to the lasting kingdom.

May Brigit save us beyond troops of demons;
may she break before us the battles of every death.

May she pay the rent sin has put on us;
the blossomed branch;
the Mother of Jesus
the dear young woman,
that I may be safe in every place
with Brigit at my side!

4
Brigit After Her Death

And from that time to this the housekeepers have a rhyme to say on Saint Brigit's day, bidding them to bring out a firkin of butter and to divide it among the working boys. For she was good always, and it was her desire to feed the poor, to do away with every hardship, to be gentle to every misery. And it is on her day the first of the birds begin to make their nests, and the blessed Crosses are made with straw and are put up in the thatch; for the death of the year is done with and the birthday of the year is come.

And this is what the people of Scotland say in a verse:

Brigit put her finger in the river
on the feast day of Brigit,
and away went the hatching-mother of the cold.

She washed the palms of her hands
in the river on the day of the feast of Patrick,
and away went the birth mother of the cold.

And this is a hymn Broccan made for Brigit:

Victorious Brigit did not want
the world to be her own;
the spending of the world was not dear to her;
the world for her was a wonderful ladder
for the people to climb
to the kingdom of the Son of Mary.

A wild boar came among her swine;
he hunted the wild pigs to the north;
Brigit blessed him with her staff,
that he made his dwelling with her own herd.

She was open in all her doings;
she was Mother of the great King's Son;
she blessed the frightened bird
till she played with it in her hand.

Before going with angels to the battle,
let us go running to Brigit;
to remember the Lord is better than any poem,
stronger than any curse.
Victorious Brigit did not want
the world to be her own.

Her Care for Leinster

On the day of the battle of Almhuin, two hundred years after her death, Brigit was seen over the men of Leinster, while Columcille was seen over the Ua Neil; and it was the men of Leinster won that battle. And a long time after that again, when Strongbow had brought great trouble into Ireland and was promised the kingdom of Leinster was near his end, he cried out from his bed that he saw Brigit of the Gael, and that it was she herself was bringing him to his death.

She Remembers the Poor

But if Brigit belonged to the east and the south, she yet is not forgotten in the west and the north, and

the people of Burren and of Corcomruadh and Kinvara go every year to her blessed well that is near
the sea, praying and remembering her. And in that
well there is a little fish that is seen every seven
years, and whoever sees that fish is cured of every
disease.

And there is a woman living yet that is poor and
old who saw that blessed fish, and this is the way
she tells the story: "I had a pearl in my eye one time,
and I went to Saint Brigit's well on the cliffs. Scores
of people there were by it, looking for cures, and
some got them and some did not get them. And
I went down the four steps to the well and I was
looking into it, and I saw a little fish no longer than
your finger coming from a stone under the water.
Three spots it had on the one side and three on
the other side, red spots and a little green with the
red, and it was very civil coming hither to me and
very pleasant wagging its tail. And it stopped and
looked up at me and gave three wags of its back,
and walked off again and went in under the stone.

"And I said to a woman that was near me that I
saw the little fish, and she began to call out and to say

there were many coming with cars and with horses for a month past and none of them saw it at all. And she tested me, asking had it spots, and I said it had, three on the one side and three on the other side.

"'That is it,' she said.

"And within three days I had the sight of my eye again. It was surely Saint Brigit I saw that time; who else would it be? And you would know by the look of it that it was no common fish. Very civil it was, and nice and wriggly, and no one else saw it at all. Did I say more prayers than the rest? Not a prayer. Was I better than the others? Not a whit. I was young in those days. I suppose she took a liking to me, maybe because of my name being Brigit the same as her own."

The Boy That Dreamed He Would Get His Health

There was a beggar boy used to be in Burren, that was very simple like and had no health, and if he would walk as much as a few yards it is likely he would fall on the road. And he dreamed twice that he went to Saint Brigit's blessed well upon the cliffs and that he found his health there. So he set out to go to the well, and when he came to it he fell in and he was drowned. Very simple he was and innocent and without sin. It is likely it is in Heaven he is at this time.

The Water of the Well

And there is a woman in Burren who now is grateful to Saint Brigit, for, she said, "I brought my little girl that was not four years old to Saint Brigit's well on the cliffs, where my girl was ailing and pining away. I brought her as far as the doctors in Gort and they could do nothing for her and then I promised to go to Saint Brigit's well, and from the time I made that promise she got better. And I saw the little fish when I brought her there; and she grew to be as strong a girl as ever went to America. I made a promise to go to the well every year after that, and so I do, of a Garlic Sunday, that is the last Sunday in July. And I brought a bottle of water from it last year and it is as cold as amber yet."

The Binding

And when the people are covering up a red sod under the ashes in the night time to spare the seed of the fire for the morning, they think upon Brigit the Fiery Arrow, and this is what they do be saying: "I save this fire as Christ saved everyone; Brigit beneath it, the Son of Mary within it; let the three angels having most power in the court of grace be keeping this house and the people of this house and sheltering them until the dawn of day."

For this is what Brigit had a mind for: lasting goodness that was not hidden; minding sheep and rising early; hospitality towards all folk. It is she who keeps everyone that is in straits and in dangers; it is she who puts down sicknesses; it is she who quiets the voice of the waves and the anger of the great sea. When a man or woman is filled with anger, ready to speak out in hate, they have only to call on Brigit, and she will heal the home. She is the All-Healer; she is the mother of the flocks; she is the Christ-bearer; she is the Mary of the Gael.

PART III

BRENDAN
THE VOYAGER

Like Patrick and Brigit, Saint Brendan was also real person. He may even have been one of the first Europeans to reach the Americas.

Brendan is believed to have been born in the year 484, in Munster in southwest Ireland. He was ordained as a priest in 512 and became one of the Twelve Apostles of Ireland, Christian elders who absorbed into themselves the Druids' role as wisdom-keepers. Brendan's vocation called him not only to a life of prayer but also to a life of constant journeying. A skilled navigator, he first sailed around Ireland's scattered islands, building monasteries wherever he could. Next, he sailed still further, to the Arran Islands, Wales, and even Brittany in France. In each place he went, he spread the news of Christ and built communities of faith and learning.

Late in his life, the story goes, Brendan heard tales of a marvelous land to the west, a land that was the original Garden of Eden and also the Paradise to which he believed all life lead. After spending time in prayer alone on the Dingle Peninsula, Brenda felt called to build a currach (a round-bottomed boat with square sails, waterproofed with skins). With a crew of Christian brothers, he set sail for the Promised Land, the Isle of the Blessed.

Brendan's story was written down in various places, including Ireland's annals and genealogies. In the eighth century, the *Navigatio Sancti Brendani* (upon which the nineteenth-century folk account contained here was based) was quite the medieval bestseller. Brendan's voyage became so well known that cartographers included his "Paradise" on their maps.

Today, some historians believe that Brendan did in fact reach the Americas. They give credence to the saint's voyage based on Viking sagas that tell of finding Christian communities in Iceland, communities founded by the Irish before the Vikings' arrival. One Scandinavian account of the Norsemen's journeys to the Americas mentions that they met with a Native group who had already seen Europeans, and some Norse accounts imply that they encountered Natives who could speak a form of Gaelic.

Less well accepted by the scholarly community are the claims from marine biologist Barry Fell that petroglyphs in West Virginia contain symbols similar to the Ogam script, the ancient Irish alphabet. According to Fells, these ancient inscriptions narrate the story of Christ's birth—but archeologists and historians have almost unanimously rejected his conclusions.

The greatest argument against the historicity of Brendan's great voyage, however, was the nature of his boat. Experts were skeptical that such a primitive craft would have been able to cross the Atlantic. In 1976, however, Tim Severin proved that Brendan could in fact have reached the Americas in his small ship. Severin built a replica of a fifth-century Irish currach, set sail from Ireland, made stops at Iceland and Greenland, and eventually, a year after he began his voyage, reached Newfoundland—using only fifth-century technology.

Of course we can never completely sort the facts from the fancy in these ancient Celtic tales. The Celts did not see the same division between "history" and "fiction" we do today. Instead, stories like Brendan's held deep emotional and spiritual meaning that was "true" at a deeper level than mere facts.

Brendan's story is a form of *immram*, a sea journey to a "hidden world." The Christian Celts' immram stories carried on a still more ancient pagan legacy of mysterious journeys to the Otherworld. These stories are all a form of what Joseph Campbell called the "hero's journey"—and according to Campbell, we each have our own journey to make.

Like Brendan, we are all "called" to venture out past our familiar boundaries, into new territories where we discover amazing treasures, learn new things, and return changed. "The big question," wrote Campbell, "is whether you are going to be able to say a hearty yes to your adventure."

When we hear the call, will be like Brendan—and make up our minds "to search out that place of joy by the help of God"?

1
The Land of Promise

Blessed Brendan was born in Ciarraige Luachra of a good father and mother. One time, when he was on Slieve Daidche beside the sea, he saw in a vision a beautiful island with angels serving upon it. And an angel of God came to him in his sleep and said, "I will be with you from now on through the length of your lifetime, and it is I who will teach you to find that island you have seen."

When Brendan heard those words from the angel, he cried as though joy had struck him a blow, and he gave great thanks to God. Then he went back to the thousand brothers that were his people.

The News of the Hidden Country

It happened now there was a young man by name of Mernoke who was a brother in another house, who went out in a ship looking for some lonely place where he might serve God. When he came to an island near to the Mountain of Stones, he liked it well and stopped there a good while, himself and his people. But after that, he put out his ship again and sailed on eastward through the length of three days. And it seemed to him on a sudden that a cloud came around them, and they were in darkness the whole of the day, till by the will of our dear Lord the cloud passed away. Then they saw before them a shining lovely island.

Joy and rejoicing were plenty in that island, and every herb was full of blossom and every tree was full of fruit. As for the ground, it was shining with precious stones on every side, and heaven itself could hardly be better.

There came to them then a very comely young man, who called every one of them by name and gave them a pleasant welcome. He said to them, "It would be right for you to give good thanks to Jesus Christ who is showing you this hidden place, for this is the country He will give to His darlings upon earth at the world's end, and it is to this place He himself will come. And there is another island besides this one," he said, "but you have not leave to go onto it or to have sight of it at all. And you have been here through the length of half a year," he said, "without meat or drink or closing your eyes in sleep."

They thought now they had not been the length of half an hour in that place, they had been so happy and so content. And he told them that this was the first dwelling place of Adam and Eve. There never came darkness there, and the name of it was the Earthly Paradise. Then he brought them back to their ship again, and when they were come to it, he vanished out of their sight, and they did not know where he went.

Then they set out over the sea again, and where they came to land was the place where Brendan and his brothers lived. They questioned Mernoke's people as to where they had been. "We have been," they said, "at the gates of Paradise, in the Land of Promise, and we had every sort of joy there and feasting, and there is always day in it and no night at all."

And their clothes had the sweetness of that place about them yet and the brothers said, "We are certain indeed you have been in that place, by the happy smell of you."

And when Brendan heard all these tidings, he stood still for a while thinking with himself. After that he went about among the brothers and chose out twelve of them that he thought more of than of all the rest. He consulted them and asked advice of them.

"Dear Father," they said, "we have left our own will and our friends and all our goods, and have come as children to you. Whatever you think well to do," they said, "we will do it."

The Beginning of Brendan's Search

So with that, Brendan made his mind up to search out that place of joy by the help of God. First, he fasted forty days and did hard penance. Then he made a very large ship, having strong hides nailed over it, and pitch over the hides, that the water would not come in.

He took his own twelve with him, and took his leave of the brothers and bade them good-bye.

Those he left behind, were sorry every one. Two among them came when he was in the ship and begged hard to go with him.

Brendan said, "You have leave to sail with me—but one of you will be sorry that he asked to come." But for all that, they were still determined to go with him.

Then they rowed out into the great sea of the ocean in the name of our Lord. The sea and the wind drove the ship at will, so that on the morning of the morrow they were out of sight of land. And so they went on through forty days, with the wind driving them eastward, but nothing daunted their spirits.

2
Adventures at Sea

At last they saw to the north a very large island having hard rocks on every side. They sailed around it for three days before they could come near any place to land. Finally, they found a little harbor and landed.

The Very Comely Hound

Then there came of a sudden a very comely hound, leaping and jumping. It fell down at Brendan's feet and bade him welcome in its own way, with its tail awag.

"Good brothers," said Brendan, "there is nothing for us to be in dread of, for I know this is a Messenger to lead us into a right place."

Then the hound brought them into a great hall where there was a table having a cloth upon it, and bread and fish. They were each one glad for it, and they sat down to eat and drink. After their supper, they found beds ready for them, and they took their fill of sleep.

The Island of Sheep

On the morrow, they went back to their ship, and they sailed a long time on the sea before they could see any land. At last, they saw before them a very green island, and when they landed and looked about them, they saw sheep on every side, the whitest and the finest that ever were seen, for every sheep was the size of an ox.

There came to them then a very well-looking old man, and he gave them a kind welcome. "This place," he said, "that you are come to is the Land of Sheep, and there is never winter here but lasting summer, and that is why the sheep are so large and so white, for the grass and the herbs are the best to be found in any place at all. And go on," he said,

"till you come by the Grace of God to a place that is
called the Paradise of Birds. It is there you will keep
your Easter."

Jasconye the Fish

Then they went into the ship again and it was driven
by storms till they saw before them another little island, and the brothers went to land on it, but
Brendan stayed in the ship. They put fish in a cauldron and lighted a fire to boil it. No sooner were
the fire hot and the fish beginning to boil, than the
island began to quake and to move like a living thing.
There was great fear on the brothers, and they went
back into the ship, leaving the food and the cauldron
behind them. Then they saw what they took to be
an island going fast through the sea, and when they
noticed the fire burning a long way off, they were
astonished.

They asked Brendan then did he know what was
that great wonder, and Brendan comforted them
and said, "It is a great fish, the biggest of the fishes of
the world. Jasconye his name is, and he is laboring

day and night to put his tail into his mouth, but he cannot do it because of his great bulk."

The Paradise of Birds

They went on then to the westward through the length of three days, and very downhearted they were to be seeing no land. But not long after, by the will of God, they saw a beautiful island full of flowers and herbs and trees, and they were glad enough to see it. They went on land and gave thanks to God.

They went a long way through that lovely country, till they came to a very good well and a tree beside it full of branches. On every branch were beautiful white birds, so many of them that not a leaf hardly could be seen. Looking at such a tree made their hearts leap with joy, and the happy singing of the birds was like the noise of Heaven.

Brendan's joy was so great he wept. He kneeled down and bade the Lord to tell him the meaning of the birds. Then a little bird of all the birds flew toward him from the tree. With the flickering of his wings, he made a very merry noise like a fiddle. It seemed to Brendan he had never heard such joyful music.

Then the little bird looked at him, and Brendan said, "If you are a Messenger, tell me your estate and why you sing to happily."

The bird said, "One time we were every one of us angels, but when our master Lucifer fell from heaven for his high pride, we fell along with him, some higher and some lower. And because our offence was but a little one," he said, "our Lord has put us here without pain in great joy and merriment to serve what way we can upon that tree. And on the Sunday that is a day of rest," he said, "we are made as white as any snow that we may praise the Holy One the better. And it is twelve months," he said, "since you left your own place, and at the end of seven years, there will be an end to your desire. And through these seven years," he said, "it is here you will be keeping your Easter until you will come into the Land of Promise."

Then the bird took his leave of them and went back to his fellows upon the tree. It was upon an Easter Day all this happened. Then all the birds began to sing the Vespers, and there could be no merrier music if God was among them.

After supper, Blessed Brendan and his comrades went to bed. They rose up on the morning of the morrow, and the birds sang the matins. They said the verses of the psalms, and sang all the Hours, as is the habit with Christians. Brendan and his people stopped there for eight weeks till after the Pentecost, and then they sailed back again to the Island of the Sheep. There they got good provision and took their leave of the old man their helper, and went back into their ship.

The Silent Brotherhood

Then the bird of the tree came to them again and he said, "You will sail from this to an island where there are four and twenty brothers, and you will spend your Christmas with those holy men." With that, he flew back again to his comrades.

Then Brendan and his people went out again into the ocean in the name of God. The winds hurled them up and down, until they were in such great danger they tired of their lives. They were tossed about through the length of four months, and they had nothing to be looking at but the sky and the waves. At last, they saw an island that was a good way off, and they cried to Jesus Christ to bring them there—but the waves rose about them another forty days, and they were loath to go on living.

They came then to a little harbor, but it was too narrow for the ship to go into it, so they cast the anchor and they swam to the land. Upon searching the island, they found two wells. The water of the one was bright and clear, but the water of the other was as if stirred and muddy. Some of them were going to drink from the wells, but Brendan bade them not to do it without leave.

Then a comely old man came to them and gave them a fair enough welcome. He kissed Brendan and led them by many good wells till they came to a great Abbey. Within it to welcome them were four and twenty brothers having royal cloaks woven of threads of gold, and a royal crown before them and candles on every side. The Abbot came and kissed Brendan very humbly and bade him and his people welcome. He led them into a beautiful hall and mixed them there among his own people.

Then there came one that served them by the will of God and gave them plenty of meat and drink. He set a good white loaf between every two, and white well-tasting roots and herbs. They drank the water of the good clear well they had first seen, but they did not know what roots those were.

Then the Abbot came and heartened them and bade them to eat and to drink their fill. "For every day," he said, "our meat and drink is brought to our cellar by a strong man; and we do not know where it is brought from but only that it is sent to us through God. We have never provided meat or drink for ourselves," he said. "Four and twenty brothers we are, and every day of the week God sends us twelve loaves, and on every Sunday and on the day of Saint Patrick twenty-four loaves, and the bread that we do not use at dinner we use it at supper-time. And now at your coming our Lord has sent us forty-eight loaves that we may be merry together. And always twelve of us go to dinner," he said, "while another twelve of us serve the quire.

We are here these fourscore years and in this country there is no sickness or bad weather. There are seven wax tapers in the quire," he said, "that have never been lighted by any man's hand, and they burn day and night at every hour of prayers. They have never wastened or lessened through these fourscore years."

After that, Brendan went to the church with the Abbot, and they said the evening prayers together very devoutly. Brendan saw beautiful woven stuffs and chalices of clear crystal, and in the quire were twenty-four seats for the twenty-four brothers and a seat for the Abbot in the middle of them all.

Brendan asked the Abbot how long it was they had kept silence so well that no one of them spoke to the others, and the Abbot said, "Our Lord knows no one of us has spoken to another these fourscore years."

When Brendan heard that, he cried for joy and said, "Dear Father, for the love of God let me stop along with you here."

"You know well," said the Abbot, "you have no leave to do that, for has not our Lord showed you what you have to do, and that you will turn back to Ireland in the end?"

And as Brendan was kneeling in the church, he saw a bright angel that came in by the window and lighted all the candles in the church. Then the angel went out by the window again to Heaven.

"There is wonder on me," said Brendan, "that those candles burn the way they do and never to waste."

"Did you never hear," said the Abbot, "how in the old time Moses saw a bush that was burning from the top to the ground, and the more it burned the greener were the leaves? So let you not wonder at these candles," he said, "for the power of the Lord is as great now as ever it was."

The Feast of the Resurrection

When Brendan had stopped there through Christmas and for Little Christmas, he bade good-bye to the Abbot and the brothers and went back to the ship with his people. The sea tumbled them up and down until they were sorry enough. When Passover came, they came again to the Island of Sheep, and they met there with the same old man as before, and he welcomed them a second time.

On Holy Thursday after supper, he washed their feet and kissed them, and they stayed in that place till Easter Eve. Then at his bidding, they set out and sailed to the place where the fish Jasconye was lying. They found upon his back the cauldron they had left there a year ago, and they kept the Feast of the Resurrection there upon the fish's back. They sang there their Matins and their Vespers and all their Masses, and the great beast stayed as still as any stone.

The Bird's Foretelling

When they had kept their Easter with great honor, they went on to the island having the tree of birds. The little bird gave them a good welcome and the sound of his song was lively indeed. So they stopped there from Easter to Candlemas the same as the year before, very happy and content, listening to the merry service that was sung upon the tree.

Then the bird told Blessed Brendan he should go back again for Christmas to the Island of the Abbey, and at Easter he should come hither again and the rest of the year he should be laboring in the great sea in trouble and in danger. "And so it will be with you from year to year to the end of forty years," be said, "and then you will reach to the Land of Promise; and then through forty days you will have your fill of joy. And after that you will return to your own country," he said, "quite easily and without any annoying, and there you will end your life."

Then the Angel that was their helper brought all sorts of provision and loaded the ship and made all ready. So they thanked our Lord for his great goodness that he had showed them so often in their great need, and they sailed out into the sea among great storms.

3
Dangers of the Sea

And soon there came after them a horrible great fish that was following their ship, casting up such great spouts of water out of his mouth that they had like to be drowned. He was coming so fast that he had all but reached them. Then they cried on Jesus Christ to help them in that great danger.

And with that there came another fish bigger than the first out of the west, and made an attack on him and beat him and at the last made three halves of him. Then the bigger fish went away again as he came, and they were very glad and gave thanks to Jesus Christ.

After that again they were very downhearted through hunger, for all their food was spent. But there came to them then a little bird having with him a great branch of red grapes, and they lived by them through fourteen days and had their fill.

Just when the grapes failed them, they came to a little island that was full of beautiful trees, with fruit on every bough of them. Brendan landed out of the ship and gathered as much of that fruit as would last them through forty days, and they went sailing and ever sailing through storm and through wind.

Of a sudden there came sailing towards them a great monster. It made an attack upon them and on their ship and had like to have destroyed them. They cried pitifully and thought themselves as good as dead—but then the little bird that had spoken with them from the tree at Easter time came at the monster and struck out one of his eyes with the first attack. With second, he struck out the other and made an end of him such that he fell into the sea. Brendan was well pleased when he saw that bird coming.

Then they gave thanks to God, and they went on sailing until Saint Peter's Day, and they sang the service in honor of the Feast. In that place the water was so clear that they could see to the bottom, and it was all as if covered with a great heap of fishes. The brothers were in dread at the sight of all the fishes, and they advised Brendan to speak softly and not to waken the fishes for fear they might break the ship.

Brendan said, "Why would you that have these two years kept the Feast of the Resurrection upon the great fish's back be in dread of these little fishes?"

With that he made ready for the Mass and sang louder than before. The fishes awoke and started up and came all around the ship in a heap, until they could hardly see the water for fishes. But when the Mass was ended, each one of the fish turned himself and swam away, and they saw them no more.

A Border of Hell

For seven days now they were going on through that clear water. There came a south wind that drove them on, and they did not know where were they going. At the end of eight days, they saw far away in the north a dark country full of stench and smoke. As the ship drew near it, they heard great blowing and blasting of bellows, and a noise of blows like thunder. They were all afeared and blessed themselves.

Soon after, there leapt up one who was all burning, but he turned away again and gave out a cry that could be heard a long way off.

With that there came demons thick about them on every side, with tongs and fiery hammers. The demons followed after them till it seemed all the sea to be one fire, but by the will of God they had no power to hurt them. Then the demons began to roar and cry, and threw their tongs at them and their hammers. At last, they turned from the ship with a sorrowful cry and went back to the place they came from.

"What are you thinking?" said Brendan, "was not this a merry happening? And we will come here no more," he said, "for that was a border of hell, and the devil had great hopes of us but he was hindered by Jesus Christ."

Then the south wind drove them farther again into the north, and they saw a hill all on fire, like as if walled in with fire, and clouds upon it. If there was much smoke in that other place, there was yet more again in this. Then one of the brothers began to cry and to moan and to say his time was come and that he could stay in the ship no longer, and with that he made a leap out of the ship into the sea. He cried and moaned so dolefully that it was a pity to hear him.

"My grief," he said, "my wretched life—for now I see my end and I have been with you in happiness and I may go with you no more forever!"

A Most Wretched Ghost

Then the wind turned and drove the ship southward through seven days, and they came to a great rock in the sea, with the sea breaking over it. On the rock was sitting a wretched ghost, naked and in great misery and pain, for the waves of the sea had so beaten his body that all the flesh was gone from it and nothing was left but sinews and bare bones. There was a cloth tied to his chin and two tongues of oxen with it, and when the wind blew, the cloth beat against his body, and the waves of the sea beat him before and behind. No one could find in any place a more wretched ghost.

Brendan bade him tell who was he in the name of God, and what he had done against God and why he was sitting there.

"I am a doleful shadow," he said, "that wretched Judas that sold our Lord for pence and I am sitting here most wretchedly. This is not my right place," he said, "but by our Lord's Grace I am brought here at certain times of the year, for I am here every Sunday and from the evening of Saturday, and from Christmas to Little Christmas and from Easter to the Feast of Pentecost and on every feast day of Our Lady; for he is full of mercy. But at other times I am lying in burning pain, and I am cursing and ever cursing the time when I was born. And I bid you for the love of God," he said, "to keep me from the devils that will be coming after me."

And Brendan said, "With the help of God we will protect you through the night. And tell me what is that cloth that is hanging from your head," he said.

"It is a cloth I gave to a leper when I was on earth, and because it was given for the love of God, it is hanging before me. But because it was not with my own pence I bought it but with what belonged to our Lord and His brothers," he said, "it is more harmful to me than helpful, beating very hard in my eyes. And those tongues that you see hanging," he said, "I gave to the priests upon earth and so they are here and are some ease to me, because the fishes of the sea gnaw upon them and spare me. And this stone that I am sitting upon," he said, "I found it lying in a desolate place where there was no use for it, and I took it and laid it in a boggy path where it was a great comfort to those that passed that way, and because of that it comforts me now. But there are but few good deeds I have to tell of," he said, "and so I have little to comfort me now. For what we give away in life is ours once more in death."

On the evening now of the Sunday there came a great troop of devils blasting and roaring. They said to Brendan, "Go from this, God's man, you have nothing to do here. Let us have our comrade and bring him back to hell for we dare not face our master and he not with us."

"I will not give you leave to do your master's orders," said Brendan, "but I charge you by the name of our Lord Jesus Christ to leave him here this night until tomorrow."

"Would you dare," said the devils, "to help him that betrayed his master and sold Him to death and to great shame?"

But Brendan laid orders on them not to annoy him that night, and they cried horribly and went away. With that, Judas thanked Blessed Brendan so mournfully that it was a pity to hear him.

On the morning of the morrow, the devils came again and cried out and scolded at Brendan. "Away with you," they said, "for our master the great devil bids us take him." And then they turned and took away with them that wretched one, quailing and trembling as he went.

4
Journey's End

Then Brendan and his people sailed through the length of three days and three nights, and on the Friday they saw before them an island.

Paul the Hermit

And when Brendan saw it, he began to sigh and to cry. "Paul the hermit is on that island," he said, "and there he has been without meat or drink these forty days."

And when they had come to land, that old hermit came to them and humbly welcomed them. His body was bare, but for his hair and his beard that covered it. And when Brendan saw him, he cried and he said, "Now I see one that lives the life of an angel rather than a man."

But Paul said, "You yourself are better than myself, for God has showed you more of His hidden things than to any other."

And Paul told them his own story and how he had been fed by an otter through forty years by the grace of God. Then the two blessed men parted from one another, and there was sorrow enough in that parting.

They went back to the ship, and they were driven towards the south by a great wind through the forty days of Lent. On Easter Eve they reached their good Helper, and he gave them good treatment as he had done before. Then he led them to the great fish, and it was upon his back they said their Matins and their Mass.

When the Mass was ended, the fish began to move and he swam out very far into the sea. A great terror was on the brothers when he did that with them being on his back, for it was a great wonder to see a beast that was the size of a whole country going so fast through the seas. But by the will of God the fish set them down in the Paradise of Birds sound and whole and left them there and went from them. They were well pleased to be in that place, and they spent their time there till after the Trinity as they had done before.

The Land of Promise

After that, they took their ship and sailed through forty days eastward. At the end of the forty days, there came a great shower of hail and then a dark mist came about them, and they were in it for a long time. Then their Helper came to them and said, "Let you be glad now and hearten yourselves for you are come to the Land of Promise."

They came out of the dark mist, and they saw to the east the loveliest country that anyone could see. Clear it was and lightsome, and there was enough in it of joy. The trees were full of fruit on every bough, and the apples were as ripe as at harvest time. They were going about that country through forty days and could see no end to it. It was always day there and never night, and the air neither hot nor cold but always in the one way. The delight that they found there could never be told.

Then they came to a river that they could not cross, but they could see beyond it the country that had no bounds to its beauty. There came to them then a young man, the comeliest that could be, and he gave them all a welcome. To Brendan he showed great honor and took him by the hand and said to him, "Here is the country you have been in search of, but it is our Lord's will you should go back again and make no delay. He will show you more of His hidden things when you will come again into the great sea. And charge your ship with the fruit of this country," he said, "and you will soon be out of the world for your life is near its end. This river you see here is the boundary," he said, "that divides the worlds, for no one may come to the other side of it while he is in life. When our Lord will have drawn everyone to Him, it is then that all will have leave to see this country, toward the world's end."

Brendan and his comrades did not fast from the fruit, but brought away what they could of it and of precious stones. They put them in their ship and went away homewards, and sorry enough they were to go.

Brendan's Homecoming

They sailed home in their ship to Ireland, and the brothers they had left behind were glad to see them come home out of such great dangers after they had been gone so many years.

As to Brendan, he was from that time as if he did not belong to this world at all, for his mind and his joy were in the delight of Heaven. He died in Ireland and was buried—and may God bring us to the same joy his blessed soul returned to!

PART IV

COLUMCILLE
FRIEND OF
THE ANGELS

On a Thursday in 521 in Ireland's County Donegal, a boy was born into the royal house of Uí Néill. He was named Crimthain, a name that meant "fox" or "cunning wolf." His birth came eighty years after the death of Saint Patrick, and by now the Celts in Ireland had been hearing the message of Jesus for several generations. Crimthain grew up as a Christian, and even as a boy, he spent so much time in prayer that he came to be called Columcille, meaning "Dove of the Church." His Latin name would be Columba.

Most of what we know about Columcille comes from an eighth-century biography, written a hundred years after his death. The author, one of Columcille's successors as an abbot of Iona, drew from oral accounts, as well as from an earlier biography that has since been lost. This earlier account of Columcille's life was written a mere forty-three years after his death; the author was also an abbot who came after him at Iona.

Although Christianity first reached the British Isles via the Roman Empire, at the time of

Columcille's life, Rome had abandoned Britain for more than a century. This allowed what is sometimes called the "Celtic church" to evolve somewhat independently from the growing political machine that was the institutionalized church of the Middle Ages. The Celtic church was never, however, a formally defined organization. Instead, it was a string of vibrant individuals and communities that stretched back and forth through the years and across the Celtic lands, forming a network of faith.

The ancient Christian Celts were known for their passionate love of God and others. Today we might accurately say that the American South is known for its hospitality, while being fully aware that not every person in the South is hospitable, and that in fact, things happen in the South that are the antithesis of hospitality. In a similar way, we tend to make generic statements about Celtic Christianity that can sometimes be contradicted by specific examples. History does in fact consistently demonstrate the Celts' affection for Nature and animals; their passion for the arts and respect for learning; and their sense that the spiritual world, the physical world, and the Otherworld of magic and faeries all flowed together. Unfortunately, the Celts' compassion and tolerance of others was not always so consistent. In Columcille's case, his devotion to books and the art of writing became an obstacle to his love for his fellow human beings.

The trouble began when he secretly made a copy of a book that was the property of his friend Finian of Movilla. When Finian discovered the copy, he demanded it be given to him as his rightful property. Columba insisted that the copy did not in any way diminish the original, and he asked the High King Diarmid to make the final judgment. The king upheld Finian's claim to the book. He handed down what may be the first recorded copyright law with these words: "To every cow her calf, to every book its copy."

Columcille may have been a dove, but he also had a hot temper. Furious that the king had ruled against him, he rallied his family and friends and went to war. In the end, Diarmid was defeated—and thousands died.

The king went to the Irish church (of which Columcille was a leading member) and asked them to excommunicate Columcille. Brendan of Birr argued for Columba (he said that despite Columcille's transgressions, the angels had not abandoned him), and Columcille's soul friend, Saint Molaisse, suggested that as penance Columcille be exiled forever from Ireland.

By this time Columcille's temper had cooled, and he was filled with sorrow and remorse. He welcomed his punishment, and in 563, with twelve companions, he set sail for Scotland, determined to do Christ's work there.

Along the way, they stopped at two islands where Ireland was still visible. Believing that his exile meant he should not be able to catch even a glimpse of the home he loved so much, Columcille sailed on to the tiny island of Iona. There he built his base for the missionary work he would do for the rest of his life, building churches and monasteries across Scotland, down into England, and beyond.

His Abby at Iona grew to be a center for education and artistic achievement. Columcille himself became known for his skill at diplomacy, and he used his spiritual authority to bring peace to the constant warfare of the day. He lived to be seventy-six, and left behind a world he had helped to change, mostly for the better, just as Patrick had changed Ireland.

1
Saint of Ireland

The lineage of Columcille was noble indeed. He had a right through his blood to the kingship of Ireland, but he put it from him for the sake of God.

The Cloak of Many Colors

Now before the birth of Columcille, his mother Eithne dreamed she was given a cloak of many colors, each one fairer than the last. As she stood on the strand, the cloak stretched out from her hands all the way to Scotland. Than Eithne dreamed that a young man came and took the cloak from her, and she sorrowed greatly at its lost. The man came yet again and said, "Do not grieve. This dream has been given to you so that you will know you are to give birth to a son who will be a wise and shining teacher, in Ireland and throughout Scotland. Be of joy and lift up your heart, for great will be your son's light to all who hear him, and his light will not be put out, even though long years upon years pass after he is no more."

The Golden Moon

Saint Finnian also had a vision before the birth of Columcille, and he saw in the vision two moons that rose up from Clonard, the one a silver moon and the other a golden moon. The golden moon went on toward the north till it lightened Scotland and the northern part of Ireland; and the silver moon went on till it stopped by the Sionnan and lightened the middle part of Ireland. Columcille now was the golden moon with his high lineage and his wisdom; and Ciaran was the silver moon with the brightness of his virtues and his pleasant ways.

Columcille was born in Gortan in the north, on a Thursday, which from that time since has been a lucky day. And indeed it was a wonderful child was born that day, Columcille son of Fedilmid son of

Fergus son of Connall Gulban son of Niall of the Nine Hostages. There was not a man of higher lineage or of greater name born of the Gael. He was brought for baptism to Cruithnechan the noble priest, who fostered him afterwards at the bidding of an angel, and angels were the ones who gave him his name.

He Learns His Letters

And when the time for reading came to him, the priest went to a knowledgeable man who was in the country and asked him when would it be right for the little lad to begin. When the knowledgeable man had looked at the sky, he said, "Write out the letters for him now." So the letters were written out upon a cake, and Columcille ate the cake, one part to the east of the water and the other part to the west of the water. And the knowledgeable man said then through his prophecy, "It is the same way the sway of this young lad will be, one half to the east of the sea in Scotland, and the other half to the west of the sea in Ireland."

his helpers the Angels

After Columcille left his fosterer, he went from place to place for a while until he came to where Saint Finnian was at Clonard, and he built a cabin there. At that time every one of the Twelve Apostles of Ireland used to take his turn to grind meal in a quern through the night, but an angel of God in heaven used to grind for Columcille. That was the honor the Lord gave him. The angels were always around him, and they helped him often from the beginning of his life until the end.

Columcille was much loved by Heaven, but his anger was quick, and it often caused him to stumble. One time after he was put out of the brotherhood for some offense, the brothers were all gathered together at Tafiltin, holding a meeting against him, when he himself came to the meeting. Saint Brendan, one of the Twelve Apostles of Ireland, rose up when he saw him coming, and when Columcille came near, he kissed him with great respect. Some of the old men in the gathering took Brendan to one side then and they were faulting him, saying, "Why did you stand up for a man who has been put out of the brotherhood and why did you kiss him?"

And Brendan said, "If you had seen today what the Lord thought fit to show to me, you would not have dishonored him who God holds in such honor."

"What was it you saw?" asked they.

"I saw," said Brendan, "a very bright pillar with fiery hair about it going before this man, and the company I saw travelling over the plain with him were the angels of God."

One night a very beautiful young man in shining clothes came to Columcille in the night time and said, "God be with you, and be strong now and steadfast, for God has sent me to keep you for ever and always amid all the sin of the world."

But Columcille was afraid, and asked him who he was.

"I am Axal," he said, "a Helper, an angel of the Lord. I am come to help you and to protect you from every danger and trouble of the world."

Throughout his life, many angels used to be coming to his help, but it is likely Axal was the one that was always at hand.

One time Columcille was sitting in his little cell, writing, when of a sudden his looks changed and he called out, "Help! help!"

Two of the brothers who were at the door asked him why he had cried out. Columcille told them that of a sudden he had seen one of the brothers falling from the highest point of a high house that was being built in Doire. "And I bade the angel of the Lord," he said, "that was just now standing among you to go to his relief. And with all the land and sea that lay between," he said, "the angel that had but left us as he began to fall was there in time to support him before he reached the ground, so that there was no hurt or bruise upon him at all. And that was wonderful help," he said, "that could be given so very quickly as that."

His Love of the Oakwood

Aedh King of Ireland gave up the house he had in Doire to Columcille, and he made his dwelling there. He had so great a love for the land, and the cutting of oak trees pained him so much, that he could not find a place where his church could be built facing the east as was the custom. Rather than fell a single oak, he had the church built with its side turned to the east instead.

He commanded those who came after him not to cut a tree. If one fell of itself or was blown down by the wind in that place, then after nine days, they might share it between the people of the townland, bad and good, a third of it to the great house and a tenth to be given to the poor.

After he was gone away to Scotland, Columcille wrote a hymn that shows there was nothing worse to him than the cutting of that oakwood:

> *Though there is fear on me*
> *of death and of hell,*
> *I will not hide*
> *that I have more fear of the sound*
> *of an axe over in Doire.*

Columcile's Little Kinsman

Baothan who was later a saint of the Gael was of the kindred of Columcille, and it was Columcille who sent him when he was a little lad to be taught by Saint Colman Ela. But although Baothan had good wits enough his memory failed him, and it was hard for him to keep in mind what his master taught him.

One day Colman was vexed with him at his task and struck him. Then Baothan went away into the wood to hide himself and to avoid his tasks. While he was there, he saw a man alone, building a house. As he came to the end of weaving one rod into the wall, he would set the head of another to it, and so he worked on from rod to rod, setting one only at a time. That seemed very tedious to the young lad till he saw the wall rising as he watched. Then he said to himself, "If I had worked at my learning as this man works at his building it is likely I might be a scholar now."

At that moment, a shower of rain fell, and he took shelter from it under an oak tree. He saw a drop of rain falling from a leaf of the tree on one spot, and he pressed his heel on that spot and made a little hollow. It was not long till the hollow was filled by the dropping of the one drop. And Baothan said then, "If I had worked at my task and my learning even little by little like that drop without doubt

I would be a scholar now. Now I make my vow," he said, "that from this out to my life's end I will never give up my learning however hard it may be to me, for little by little great things are done."

His Farewell to Aran

Columcille made a round of the whole of Ireland and he sowed the faith and did what he had to do. Before he went to Scotland, he stopped in Aran of the Saints for a while, and there is a spot in the island where he used to be walking that is always green to this day. And when he left Aran he made this complaint:

> A farewell from me to Aran;
> a sorrowful farewell as I think;
> I myself sent eastward to Iona,
> and the sea between it and Aran.

> A farewell from me to Aran;
> it is it that vexes my heart;
> I not to be westward on her waves
> among troops of the saints of heaven.

A farewell from me to Aran;
my faithful heart is vexed;
it is a lasting leave taking;
Och! this parting is not of my will.

A farewell from me to Aran;
it is that is the sorrowful parting;
she to be full of white angels
and I without a lad in my currach.

Och it is far, Och it is far
I am put away from Aran in the west;
sent out towards the hosts of Mona
to visit the men of Scotland in the east.

The Son of God, O, the Son of God,
it is He sent me out to Iona;
it is He gave, great the profit,
Aran as the dwelling-place
of prayers and of teaching.

Aran my sun, O Aran my sun,
my affection is lying in her to the west;

it is the same to be under her clean earth
as under the earth of Paul and Peter.

Aran my sun, O Aran my sun,
my love is lying in her to the west;
to be within the sound of her bell,
it is the same thing as to be in happiness.

Aran my sun, O Aran my sun,
my love is lying in her to the west;
whoever goes under her clean earth,
the eye of no bad thing will see him.

Blessed Aran, O blessed Aran,
it is a pity for anyone that is against Aran;
it is what he will get on the head of it,
shortening of life and the grave.

Blessed Aran, O blessed Aran,
it is a pity for him that is against Aran;
wasting on his children and on his cattle;
he himself in bad case at the end.

Blessed Aran, O blessed Aran,
it is a pity for anyone that is against you;
angels coming down from Heaven
to visit you every day of the week.

Gabriel comes every Sunday
as it is Christ gave the order;
fifty angels, not weak the cause
putting a blessing on her.

Every Monday, O every Monday,
Michael comes, great the advantage;
thirty angels, good their behavior,
come blessing her.

Every Tuesday, O every Tuesday,
Raphael comes, of high power
to give a blessing on her houses,
attending on the prayers of Aran.

Hard Wednesday, O hard Wednesday,
Urial comes, great the advantage;
he comes to bless three times
over the high angelic trees.

Every Thursday, O every Thursday,
Sariel comes, great the advantage;
dividing God's good increase
from heaven on the bare stones.

Every Friday, O every Friday,
Ramael comes, his ranks with him;
the way every eye is satisfied
with white, very bright angels.

Mary comes, Mother of God,
having her women in her keeping;
angels are in their company;
they bless Aran every Saturday.

If there was no other life
but listening to the angels of Aran,
it would be better than any life under heaven
to be hearing their talk together!

After he went over the sea, he also wrote this verse of Doire, showing that his heart never left the oakwood there:

It is delightful to be on Beinn Edair
before going over the white sea;
the beating of the waves against its wall;
the bareness of its border and its strand.

It is great is the swiftness of my currach
and its back turned to Doire
it is a fret to me my journey over the high sea,
traveling to Scotland of the ravens.

My foot in my sweet-sounding currach;
my sorrowful heart pleading.
It is a weak man that is not a leader;
all that are without knowledge are blind together.

There is a grey eye
that is looking back upon Ireland;
it will never see from day to day
the men or the women of Ireland.
I stretch my sight over the salt waters
from the strong oaken planks;
there is a great tear in my eye

when I look back on Ireland;
my mind is set upon Ireland,
on Loch Lene of Magh Line
on the country of the men of Ulster;
on smooth Munster and on Meath.

Plentiful in the west are the apples;
plentiful the kings and the makings of kings;
plentiful the wholesome sloes;
plentiful the oaks with acorns.

Sweet voiced her clerks;
sweet voiced her birds;
her young men gentle, her old men wise;
her great men are good to look at;
her women noble.

Take my blessing with you, beautiful boy,
my blessing and my benediction.
Take my blessing over the sea
to the nobles of the island of the Gael;
let them not give heed to their enemy's words,
or to his threat of harming them.

Take my blessing with you to the west;
my heart is broken in my body.
If death should overtake me suddenly
it is through great love of the Gael.

Gael, Gael, dear dear name
my one shout and my call!
Dear is soft haired Cuimin,
dear are Caindech and Comgall.

If I had the whole of Scotland
from the middle out to the borders
I would sooner have a place and a house
in the middle of pleasant Doire.

It is the reason I love Doire,
for its quietness for its purity;
it is quite full of white angels
from the one end to the other.

It is the reason I love Doire,
for its quietness for its purity;
quite full of white angels
is every leaf of the oaks of Doire.

My Doire my little oakwood,
my dwelling and my white cell;
O living God in heaven,
it is a pity for him that harms it!

Dear are Durrow and Doire;
dear is Rathboth in its whiteness;
dear is Druimhome of delicate fruits;
dear are Sord and Cenacles.

Dear to my heart in the west Druimciab
at the strand of Culcinne;
to see white Loch Febhail,
the shape of its harbor is delightful.

Delightful is that and delightful is the sea
where the gulls are crying;
going a long way from Doire
it is quiet and it is delightful!

2
The Island of Iona

And when Columcille left Ireland for Scotland, he did good service there, for he brought many of the folk of Scotland to the light of Christ. It was to the island of Iona he went first, and when he reached to it he said to his people, "It would be well for us to put roots into the earth in this place. And there is leave for one of you," he said, "to go under the earth of this island to consecrate it."

Odhran rose up quickly then and said, "I am ready for that if you will take me."

"You will get your reward for that, Odhran," said Columcille, "for no asking will be granted to anyone at this place unless he will ask it first of you."

Then Odhran joined the company of Heaven, and after that Columcille laid the foundation of his church. Odhran worked for the church in Heaven, while Columcille and his brothers did their work on the earth.

Columcille bade the brothers to have a mind prepared for red martyrdom—in other words, ready to bleed and die—with a mind strong and steadfast for white martyrdom, a total surrender to God. He taught them to have forgiveness from the heart for everyone, and to be in constant prayer for all that troubled them. "And let you be as much in earnest saying the office for the dead," he said, "as if every one of the faithful dead was your own near friend."

But if it was in Iona he had his dwelling-place, he went every Thursday to Heaven at the call of the God of the Three.

The Crane from Ireland

One time when Columcille was living in the island of Iona, he called to one of the brothers and said, "In the morning of the third day from this, go down and waft on the shore to the west of the island, for at the ninth hour there will come a stranger, a crane from the north part of Ireland, that has been driven here and there by winds. It will lie down on the strand, tired and worn out. Bring it into some neighboring house," he said, "where it will get a welcome, and where you can be minding it and feeding it for three days and three nights. And when it is refreshed," he said, "with the three days' rest and has no mind to stay longer with us, it will fly back to the pleasant part of Ireland it came from. I give this bird to your special care," he said.

The brother did as Columcille bade him and tended the crane. At the end of the third day, the crane rose to a great height in the air and stopped for a little while, marking out its path to its home. Then it went back across the sea to Ireland, as straight as it could fly on a calm day.

And Columcille longed to fly with it, for Ireland was more to him than any other place. Columcille made this hymn one time, praising Ireland:

It would be delightful, Son of my God,
to travel over the waves of the rising flood;
over Loch Neach, over Loch Febhail,
beyond Beinn Eigne,

*the place we used to hear
fitting music from the swans.
The host of the gulls would make a welcome
with their sleepy music if my currach,
the Red Dewy One, should come
to the harbor of joyous sorrow.*

*I have my fill of riches if I thought it enough,
wanting Ireland, in the strange country
where I have chanced and I tired.
It is a pity the journey that was put upon me,
O King of mysteries!*

*It is happy the son of Dima is
when he is listening in Durrow
to the desire of his mind;
the sound of the wind against the elms;
the laughter of the blackbird clapping his wings;
to listen at break of day
to the lowing of the cattle in Rigrencha,
to listen at the brink of summer
to the cry of the cuckoo from the tree.*

There are three things dearest to me
on the whole of this peopled world,
Doire and Doire-Ethne and Doire
the high country of angels.
My visit to Comgall, my feast with Cainnech,
it is they were honey sweet to me.
I have loved Ireland of the waters,
all that is in it, but not its government.

The Poor Man and the Stake

There came to Columcille one time a poor man of Scotland who was in great misery and had no way of living. When Columcille had given him all he had to give of alms, he said to him, "Go now into that wood beyond and bring me a branch from it."

The poor man did as Columcille bade him and brought the branch. Columcille took it, made a sharp point on it, and he gave it back to the poor man, saying, "Take good care of the stake and so long as you have it, you will never be without plenty of venison in the house. But it will not harm men or cattle," he said, "but only wild creatures, beasts and fishes."

The poor man was well pleased when he heard that, and as he went home, he fixed the stake in a lonely place where the wild creatures of the wood used to be going. At the early light of the morrow, he went to look at the stake, and he saw a very large stag had fallen upon it and it had gone through him.

From that time, not a day would pass but he would find a stag or a doe or some other wild creature fixed upon the stake. In this way, his house was full of meat, and all that himself and his wife and his children could not use he would sell it to the neighbors.

But after a while, his wife said to him, "Take out that stake out of the ground, for if men or cattle should chance to fall upon it, yourself and myself and our children would be put to death or we would be led into bondage." She spoke not as a wise woman but as a woman who had lost her sense.

"That will not happen," said the husband, "for when the holy man blessed the stake, he said it would never harm folk or cattle."

But for all that he argued, in the end he did as his wife bade him. In his folly, he took the stake out of the ground and put it against the wall.

Not long after that, his house dog fell upon it and was killed. His wife said to him then, "One of the children will be the next to fall upon it and be killed."

So when she said that, he took the stake out of the house, and brought it to a very large wood and put it in the thickest of the scrub where as he thought no beast could be harmed by it. But when he came back next day, he saw a deer had fallen upon it and got its death. So he brought the stick away from there and thrust it in under the water by the edge of a river; the next day he found on it a salmon so big that he was hardly able to lift it out of the river to bring it home. Next, he brought the stake up from the river and put it outside on the roof of his house. This time, it was not long till a crow got its death by it, when it was coming to perch on the house. Upon that, the foolish man gave in to the advice of his wife and took down the stake from the roof and took an axe and cut it in a great many pieces and threw it in the fire.

After doing that, he that had been rich fell into poverty again. For the rest of their lives, all he and his wife and his children could do was to fret after the stake the blessed man had given him. They had only themselves to thank, for with their own two hands and because of their fear, they had thrown away the blessing that had been given them.

The Nettle Broth

One time Columcille was making his rounds in Iona and he saw an old woman cutting nettles to boil down for food.

"What is the cause of that misery?" said Columcille. "Why have you nothing to eat but nettles?"

"O dear father," she said, "I have one cow only and she is in calf. Nettles are what serve me through the time of waiting for milk."

When Columcille heard that, he made his mind up he would eat no other thing than broth of nettles so long as his life would last. "For if it is waiting for the one cow this woman is, in this great hunger," he said, "it would be more fitting for us to be in hunger, for we ourselves are waiting for, the everlasting kingdom." Then he said to his cook, "Bring me broth of nettles every night and bring no milk with it."

"I will do that," said the cook. But the cook bored a hole through the stick he stirred the broth with, till it was like a pipe, and he used to pour the juice of meat down through the pipe so that it was mixed with the broth. That kept a good appearance on Columcille.

The brothers saw by his looks he was well nourished and they were talking about it among themselves. And when Columcille overheard them, he said to the cook, "What is it you are giving me?"

"You know well yourself," said the cook. "If it does not come through the iron of the pot or through the stick the broth is mixed with, I know of no other thing in it but only nettles."

"That there may be good luck and a good appearance to those that come after you for ever," said Columcille.

But for all that his cook did his best, Columcille lost flesh till the track of his ribs used to be seen on the sand when he used to lie on the strand through the night time.

His Strange Visitor

One time Columcille was at Cam Eolairg on Loch Febhail, when there came a beautiful young man to him having a golden shoe upon his foot. It was only one shoe, but whatever foot he would put down on it, the shoe used to be there, so that he only needed the one.

"Where do you come from young man?" asked Columcille.

"I am Mongan son of Fiachra," said the young man, "and I am come from countries unknown and countries known. I am come," he said, "to compare my knowledge and wisdom with your own, and to know from you the place where knowledge and ignorance were born, the place where they die, and the place of their burying."

"Well then, I have a question for you," said Columcille. "What did this loch we are looking at used to be in the old time?"

"I know that," said the young man. "It was yellow, it was blossoming, it was green, it was hilly, it was a place of drinking, it had silver in it and chariots. I went through it when I was a deer before deer, when I was a salmon, when I was a very strong seal, when I was a wild dog. When I was a man I bathed in it, I carried a yellow sail, a green sail, it drowned a red sail under blood, women called out to me. Though I do not know father or mother, I speak with the living and the dead."

Then Columcille said to him, "What is there beneath those islands to the west of us?"

The young man said, "There are underneath them tuneful long-haired men, well-shaped people both men and women; there are cattle, white, red-eared, their lowing is sweet; there are herds of deer, there are good horses; there are the two-headed, there are the three-headed, in Europe, in Asia, in an unknown green country from its border to its river mouth."

"That is enough so far," said Columcille. Then he went apart with the young man to ask him the secrets of Heaven and earth. They were talking together from one hour on that day to the same hour on the next day, while Columcille's people watched them from a long way off.

When the talk came to an end, they saw the young man vanishing from them all of a minute, and no one could tell where he went. When they asked Columcille to give them news of his talk, he said that he could not tell them one word of all he had heard; and he said it was a right thing for men not to be told of it.

3
Doings in Columcille's Day

While Columcille lived on this earth, many were the doings of those who lived around him, both in Ireland and in Scotland. Often they called on Columcille, and often they offered to him, and often he blessed them.

The Breaking of Columcille's Guarantee

Fergal King of Ireland that was of the lineage of the Ua Neills of the north was gathering his people one time to go against the men of Leinster. And a long time they took coming together, for every man that was called in Conn's half of Ireland used to say, "If Donnbo goes with the army I will go."

Donnbo now was the son of a widow-woman belonging to the men of Ross, and he had never gone away from his mother's house for even one day or for one night. There was not one in all Ireland more comely or better in face and in shape than himself. He was the best at singing merry verses and telling royal stories of all in the whole world; the best to ready horses or to rivet spears or to plait hair; the best in quickness of mind and in generosity. His mother would not let him go out at the king's bidding till she got the security of Columcille that he would come back to her in safety.

So he went out with the king's army, and they went on till they came to Almhuin and there they made their camp. Then Fergal said to Donnbo, "Make mirth for us, Donnbo, for you are the best of all the musicians of Ireland at pipes and at harps and at poems, and at the old stories and the royal stories of Ireland. On the morning of tomorrow," he said, "we will give battle to the men of Leinster."

"Och," said Donnbo, "I am not able to make sport for you this night or to do any of those things that you say. But wherever you may be on the night of tomorrow," he said, "I will make amusement for you if I am living. And let the king's buffoon make sport for you tonight."

So Ua Maighlinne the king's buffoon was called, and he began his stories of the battles and the triumphs of Leinster from the destruction of Dind Righ down to that time. But no one got much sleep that night because of their great dread of the men of Leinster, and because of a storm that arose (for that was the eve of the feast of Saint Finian in the winter).

The battle was fought the next morning, and the men from the north were beaten. Nine thousand of them went to their death, and Fergal the king among them. And Ua Maighlinne fell into the hands of one of the men of Leinster, who bade him give his buffoon's roar, and he did that. His head was cut off then, but the roar was heard in the air through the length of three nights and three days, and it has stayed with the buffoons of Ireland to this day.

And as to Donnbo, he lost his life defending the king, and his head was struck off, as was the king's head.

The same night, the men of Leinster were drinking wine and making merry, and every one telling the deeds he had done in the battle. And Murchad son of the king of Leinster said, "I would give a good chariot and my own dress to any man that would go to the place of the battle and would bring me a token from it."

"I will go," said a Munster man that was among them. So he put on his battle dress and went, and when he came to the place where King Fergal's body was, he heard said as if in the air these words: "Here is a command to you from the King of the Seven Heavens: make music tonight for your master Fergal the king; though all of you have fallen here, pipers and trumpeters and harpers. Let no terror or no weakness keep you from making music for Fergal."

Then the messenger heard the music of singers and trumpeters and pipers and harpers, all sorts of music he heard, and he never heard better before or after. Then from a bunch of rushes near him, he heard a very wild song, the sweetest of all the music of the world. He went toward the rushes then, but a voice said from among them, "Do not come near me."

"Who are you?" said the messenger.

"I am the head of Donnbo," it said, "and I made a bond to make amusement for the king tonight. So do not hinder me."

"Where is Fergal's body?" said the messenger."

"It is shining there before you," said the head.

"Let me bring you away along with him," said the messenger, "for it is yourself I would sooner bring away."

"I would not wish any person to bring me away," said the head, "unless it might be Christ the Son of God. And give me the guarantee of Christ now that you will bring me back to my body again."

"I will bring you surely," said the messenger. Then he went back to where the men of Leinster were drinking yet.

"Have you a token with you?" said Murchad."

"I have," said he, "the head of Donnbo."

"Set it up on that post," said Murchad.

Then they all knew it to be the head of Dunnbo, and they all said, "It is a pity for you, Donnbo, it is comely your face was! And make amusement for us tonight," they said, "the same as you did yesterday for your lord."

Then he turned his face to the wall of the house so that it would be darker for him, and he raised his wild song. It was the sweetest of all the music on the whole ridge of the world. All the men of Leinster were crying and lamenting, with the sorrow and the softness of that song.

And when the head fell silent and still, yet they could hear the music, but wilder and sweeter than before, for now Donnbo was in Heaven.

And his mother, hearing the song, knew her son was dead, and wroth she was with Columcille for making a promise he could not keep.

The Voyage of Snedgus

One time Snedgus and Mac Riaghta, clerks that were of the people of Columcille, got into their currach of their own will, and went out over the sea on a pilgrimage. They turned righthandways, and the wind brought them northwestward into the outer ocean.

And at the end of three days, a great longing and a great thirst came upon them that they could not bear. Christ took pity on them and brought them to an island where there was a stream that had the taste of new milk, and they were satisfied with it. They gave thanks to God then and they said, "Let us leave our voyage to God, and let us put the oars in the boat."

From then on, they let the rudder alone and they put their oars in the boat. The current brought them to another island with a silver fence over the middle of it, and a fish weir. The weir was a plank of silver, and there were big salmon, every one the size of a bull-calf, leaping against the weir. And the clerks were satisfied with them.

After that they went to another island and in that island they found fighting-men having heads of cats on them. One man of the Gael was among them, and he came down to the strand and bade them welcome, saying, "A boat's crew of us came here, and there is not one left of it now but myself, for the rest of us were made an end of by the strangers of this island." He put provision into the boat for them then, and they left a blessing and took a blessing with them.

After that, the wind brought them to an island where there was a great tree, and beautiful birds in it; and on the top of the tree was a bird having a head of gold and wings of silver. She told them stories of the beginning of the world; she told them of the birth of Christ from Mary Virgin, and of His baptism and His passion. Then all the birds beat their sides with their wings till blood dropped from them, with the dread at the story of His death, and it is a very precious thing that blood was. Then the bird told of His rising again; and she told news of His coming; and all the birds burst into song like unto the angels'.

The bird gave to the clerks a leaf of the leaves of that tree, and it was the size of the hide of a great ox. Neither leaf nor stem of that tree ever withers. And she bade them to put that leaf on Columcille's altar, and it is to Kells it was brought afterwards. The music of those birds was sweet, singing psalms and praising the Lord, for they were the birds of the Plain of Heaven.

Then they bade farewell to the birds, and they went on to a very fearful country where there were men with the heads of dogs and manes of cattle. By God's good order, a clerk came to them out of the island to relieve them, for they were in a bad way for the want of food; he gave them fish and wine and wheat. Then they went on till they came to a country where the man had the heads of pigs; and there were a great many reapers reaping the corn in the middle of the summer.

From there they went on in their boat, and sang their psalms and prayed to God, till they came to a country where there were people of the Gael; and the women of that island sang a sweet strain to the clerks. One of them said, "Sing on, for this is the music of Ireland."

"Let us go to the house of the King of the island," said the women to them then, "and you will get a welcome and good treatment."

So they went into the house, and the King gave a welcome to the clerks. They rested themselves there and he asked them what was their lineage. "We are of the men of Ireland," they said, "of the people of Columcille."

"How is Ireland now?" said the King, "and how many of the sons of Domnall are living yet?"

"There are three sons of Domnall living, and Fiachna son of Domnall fell by the men of Ross. For that deed two sixties of them were put out upon the sea."

"That story is true indeed," said the King, "for it is I myself who killed the son of Domnall king of Teamhuir and we are the men who were put out on the sea. And it is well that happened for us," he said, "for here we will be till the time of our judgment. We have grown good here, without sin," he said. "The island where we are has made us good with its goodness, for here are Yew and Enoch as well. And where Yew lives is a place lifted up to heaven."

"We would like well to see Enoch," said the clerks.

"He is in a hidden place till we all go to battle on the Day of Judgment," said he. And there was another thing he said to them: "There are two lakes in this country, a lake of water and a lake of fire. Both would have gone over Ireland long ago without Martin and Patrick praying for the Gael."

Then they went on from that country, and they were in the shouting of the waves for a long time till they were tired out they were. Then great relief came to them from God, as they saw a great high island and everything that was in it was beautiful and holy. The king who lived in that island was holy and just, and his army was great, and his dwelling place was noble, for there were a hundred doors in that house and an altar at every door and a dear man at every altar offering the body of Christ. The two clerks went into the house and each of them blessed the other. After that, the whole host, women and men, went to communion at the Mass.

Then wine was given out to them and the King said, "Tell the men of Ireland that a great vengeance is going to fall upon them across the sea and your enemies will make war on you and you will live in the half of the island. And this is what brings this vengeance upon them," he said, "the great neglect they show to the testament of God and to His teaching. And for a month and a year," he said, "you will be on the sea, but you will land safely at the last, and then tell out all your news to the people of Ireland."

4

Columcille Comes to the End of His Life

Great were the deeds of Columcille, and his wisdom spread far and near, and he taught many to know the Gospel. Always his heart longed for Ireland, but he grew old in Scotland.

The Ladder of Glass

One time Columcille went to Monaster Boite and it is there his staff struck against the ladder of glass by which Boite had gone up to heaven; and he showed where his grave was and marked out his church. Three hundred churches he marked out, and he wrote three hundred books. And among the churches he left there were a hundred that had the waves for a neighbor.

A Hymn Columcille Made and He Going on a Journey

Columcille made this hymn the time the King of Teamhuir had given an order to take him, but the justice of God threw a mist about him so that his way would not be known as he went out. And it is a protection to anyone that will say it as he goes on his way.

It is alone I am on the mountain,
O King-Sun of the lucky road,
there is nothing for me to be in dread of.
If I had three score hundreds of armies
that would defend the body,
when the day of my death comes
there is no strong place wilt hold out against it.

He that is spent may get his death in a church
or in the island in the middle of the lake;
he that has God's hand with him,
his life will be safe in the front of a battle.

*There is no one could put an end to me
though he should chance upon me in danger;
there is no one could protect me
the day my life will come to its end.*

*My life, I leave it to the will of God.
There will be nothing wanting to it;
there will be nothing added to it.*

*He that is in health falls into sickness;
he that is out of his health grows sound again;
he that is in misery gets right again;
he that is in good order falls into misery.*

*Whatever God has settled for any person,
he will not leave the world until he meets it;
although a high head goes looking for more,
he will not get the size of a grain of it.*

*A man may bring a guard with him on his road;
but what guard has ever kept a man from his death?*

There is no son of a man who knows
for whom he is making a gathering;
if it is for himself or for some other one.

Leave out scarceness for a while;
it is better for you to mind hospitality.
The Son of Mary will prosper you
when every guest comes to his share.

It is often the thing that is spent
comes back again,
and the thing that is kept,
though it is not spent it vanishes away.

O living God!
It is a pity for him that does any bad thing!
The thing that is not seen comes to him;
the thing that he sees goes away out of his hand.

It is not with chance our life is;
or with the bird on the top of the twig;
or with the trunk of a crooked tree.
It is better to put our trust in the Father,
the One, and the Son.

We share every evening in the house of God,
it is what my King has made.
He is the King that made the body;
He will not let me go wanting tonight.

I do not hold to the voice of birds,
or any luck on the earthly world,
or chance or a son or a woman.
Christ the Son of God is my Druid;
Christ the Son of Mary
the great Abbot;
the Father, the Son, and the Holy Spirit.
My estates are with the King of Kings."

Columcile Keeps the Feast of Pentecost

And at last one day in the month of May, Columcille went on a cart to see the brothers that were ploughing in the north of the island of Iona; and he was comforting them and teaching them.

"Well," he said, "at the Easter that went into the month of April I was ready to go to Heaven, but I had no mind to have you sorrow or trouble after your heavy work, and so I have stayed with you from Easter to Pentecost."

When his people heard those words, they were very downhearted. Columcille turned his face westward and blessed the island, and drove away from it every bad thing. Then he came to his cell, and it was not long till there came the end of the Sabbath and the beginning of Sunday. And when he lifted his eyes, he saw a great brightness, and an angel of God waiting there above him.

After that he went out, and with him his servant Diarmuid, whose life he had lengthened with his prayers one time when he was sick. Columcille blessed the barn and two heaps of winnowed wheat that were in it. Then he told Diarmuid he had a little secret word to tell him, that on this very night of the Sabbath of rest he would go to his own rest, on the invitation of the Lord Jesus. And he sat down on the edge of the path, for all the length of his years came upon him then, and heavy they felt on his shoulders.

There came to him the old spent white horse that carried the milk vessels from the cowshed in the island to the brothers, and it cried tears into

Columcille's breast till his clothes were wet. Diarmuid would have driven the old horse away, but Columcille said, "Leave him, Diarmuid, till he cries his fill, keening me. For you are a man having reason," he said, "and you know nothing of the time of my death but what I myself have told you. But as to this beast that is without reason, God Himself has made known to him in some way that his master is going to leave him." And he gave his blessing to the horse then, and he went away at last, very sorrowful but at peace.

On the night of the Sunday of Pentecost, Columcille was the first in the church, and he knelt and prayed. The brothers came in with their candles, but the whole church was full of light, and Columcille opened his eyes wide and looked about him on every side with a great blush in his face. They knew then he was looking at the angels. The light of the angels filled the church on every side, and he blessed the brothers.

Then the life went from his body, and the household of heaven shouted its welcome. Some say that before he died, his body became that of a young man again, because he had requested Axal the angel one time that he might die in his youth. "For in old age," he said, "the body is ugly." And the angel granted him that and many other things.

How the News Was Brought to Ireland

At the hour of his death, the fishermen that were out trying for fish in the deep holes of the river Finn saw a great light to the east that lighted up the whole of the sky. The light of the angels was seen, and their hymns were heard in the high air. And at the same time the poets of Ireland were gathered at the yew tree at the head of Baile's Strand in Ulster, and they were making up stories. Forgaill, a man of Connacht and of high lineage, was the chief of all those poets, and news that Columcille was dead was brought to him by an angel riding a speckled horse.

Forgaill's Lament

This now is the poem of praise and of lamentation that was made for Columcille, Speckled Salmon of the Boinne, High Saint of the Gael, by Forgaill that was afterwards called Blind Forgaill, Chief Poet of Ireland:

It is not a little story this is;
it is not a story about a fool it is
it is not one district that is keening
but every district,
with a great sound that is not to be borne,
hearing the story of Columcille,
without life, without a church.

It is not the trouble of one house,
or the grief of one harpstring;
all the plains are heavy,
hearing the word that is a wound.

What way will a simple man tell of him?
Even Nera from the Sidhe could not do it;
now he is hidden away from us.
He that used to keep us living is dead;
he that was our rightful head has died from us;
he has died from us, that was God's messenger.

The knowledgeable man
that used to put fear from us is not here;
the teller of words does not return to us;
the teacher is gone from us
that taught silence to the people.

The whole world was his;
it is a harp without its strings;
it is a church without its abbot.

Colum rose very high
the time God's companies rose to meet him;
it is bright the angels were, attending on him.

It is short his life was, it is little used to satisfy him;
when the wind blew the sheet
against him on the sand,
the shape of his ribs could be seen through it.

He was the head of every gathering;
he was a bell of the book of the law;
he put a flame in the district of the north,
he lightened the district of the west;

the east was his along with it;
though he did not open his heart to every company.
Good was his death;
he went with God's angels
that came to meet him.

He has reached to Axal of his help
and to the troops of the archangels;
he has reached to a place where night is not seen;
he has reached to a plain
where music is always present;
where no one listens to oppression.
The King of priests has done away with his troubles.

He knew the way he was going;
he gave kindness for hatred; he learned psalms;
he broke the battle against hunger.

He knew seasons and storms;
he read the secrets of the great wisdom;
he knew the course of the moon;
he took notice of its race with the branching sun.
He was skilful in the course of the sea;

to tell every high thing we have heard from Colum,
would be to count the stars of heaven.

A healer of the heart of the wise;
a full satisfier of guests;
our crowned one who spoke with Axal;
a shelter to the naked;
a comforter to the poor;
high was his death.
We hope great honor will be given to him
on the head of these deeds."

And when Forgaill had made that lament he said, "It is a great shaping and a great finish I have given to these words, and I cannot make a praise beyond this, for my eyes have been taken from me."

Columcille's Burying Place

It is an old saying in Ireland that though Columcille died in Iona, his soul is in Doire and his body under a flagstone in Ardmacha beside Brigit and Patrick. The people of Ireland say to this day that when he was dying, he bade the brothers to put his body in a currach and to cut directions on a stick and to put the currach out to sea. So they did that and the currach floated to the north of Ireland.

A few cows had pasture near the sea, and one of them used to be going down to the shore every day, licking a brown stick that was lying there. The boy who was minding them took notice that the milk that cow gave was three times more than the milk of every other cow, and he wondered to see the cow that was the scarcest of all giving milk and butter like that and it eating nothing, but only licking a bit of a stick. So the others went and looked at the stick, and they read on it that Saint Columcille's body was in the currach and they found it there; whether it was only his bones they found, or whether he was embalmed, being such a great man, is not known. And the writing on the stick said he was to be buried in Ardmacha, between Saint Patrick and Saint Brigit. They did not know where those graves were, but they brought the body to Ardmacha, and the ground opened of itself. Then they knew it was to let him rest between those two that it had opened.

Columcille's Valley

Bran, long long ago, the hound of Finn son of Cumhail, stopped one time at the hunting, and would not follow a deer through a certain valley. And it was always said she knew that to be a valley Columcille would bless in the time to come.

The people of Slieve Echtge say there will be a great war yet in the whole world and in Ireland, and the want will be so great that the father will disown his son and will not let him in at the door. There will be great fighting on Slieve-nan-Or, the Golden Mountain, and in the Valley of the Black Pig. When the war comes as far as the blessed bush at Kilchriest, a priest will put on his stole, and will read from his book, and lift a chalice three times, and that will weaken it for a while. But the fighting will never reach to the Valley of Columcille. Those who live in that valley at the time of the last great war will be safe, for Columcille's blessing lingers there forever.

5
The Hymns of Columcille

When Columcille was yet a young man in Ireland, he studied there with the bard Gemman, and skilled he was with verse and tune. Many are the hymns he wrote throughout his life, and some are sung still on earth, and all are sung in Heaven.

High Creator

The High Creator, Ancient of Days and Unbegotten,
was without origin, without end;
The Creator is and shall be to ages of ages, infinite,
with whom is Christ the only begotten
and the Holy Spirit,
coeternal in the everlasting glory of the Godhead.
Yet we set forth not three gods,
but One God only,
saving us in three glorious Persons.

By the divine powers of the great God
is suspended the earth,
and thereto is set the circle of the great deep
supported by the strong hand of God Almighty,
promontories and rocks
with columns like bars solid, sustained
immoveable like so many strengthened foundations.

Helper of Workers

I beg that me, a little man
trembling and most wretched,
rowing through the infinite storm of life,
Christ may draw after Him to the lofty
most beautiful haven of life.

Father, Do Not Allow

Father, do not allow thunder and lightening,
lest we be shattered by its fear and fire.
All songs praise You throughout the host of angels.
Let the summits of heaven, too,
praise You with roaming lightening,

O most loving Jesus, O righteous King of Kings.
The flame of God's love dwells in my heart
As a jewel of gold is placed in a silver dish.

A Prayer of Columcille

That I might bless the Lord
whose angels watch over all;
Heaven with its countless bright orders,
land, strand, and flood,
that I might search in all the books
that would help my soul;
at times kneeling to the Heaven of my heart,
at times singing psalms,
at times contemplating the King of Heaven,
Chief of the Holy Ones;
at times at work without compulsion,
this would be delightful.
At times plucking seaweed from the rocks,
at other times fishing;
at times distributing food to the poor,
at times in a hermitage.
Let me say my daily prayers,

sometimes chanting, sometimes quiet,
always grateful to the good God.
Delightful it is to live
on a peaceful isle, in a quiet cell,
serving the King of kings

PART V

THE VOYAGE
OF MAELDUNE

You might think of *The Voyage of Maeldune* as an ancient fantasy story, created by an eighth-century version of J. R. R. Tolkien or George R. R. Martin. The long-ago storyteller let his fancy run wild. He described enormous insects, a creature whose skin whirled around its bones, pigs that breathed fire, and a magical cat. As Maeldune and his comrades sail from island to island, each one is stranger than last. On one, the very air makes everyone weep and sorrow, while on another, everyone is laughing. On yet another, time is out of joint with the rest of the world. All ancient Celtic tales are filled with forays into the supernatural world, but Maeldune's story goes somewhere else as well, into a world that is clearly the realm of one individual's imagination.

Fantasy fiction gives us opportunities to step outside the box of the "real world." It stretches our imaginations, allowing us to see past our cultural paradigms. When we return from these imaginary realms, we may find that we see ourselves and everything around us from a new angle—a fresh perspective that allows us to learn and grow. This was Maeldune's experience as well.

When A. E. Marling, a guest blogger on the Fantasy Book Critic site,[1] polled two hundred and some fantasy readers, he found these reasons why people today enjoy reading fantasy fiction:

- The opportunity to encounter the *numinous*, which Marling defines as "the tingling sensation of entering the unknown. A glittering mist of a forbidden valley, a rush down our spine as we enter a crystal cavern. It's the sense that you're entering a sacred place, ripe with otherworldly presence and mystery."
- *Entertainment*, pure and simple.
- *Adventure*.
- *Freedom* from the real world's depressing demands and limitations. "Fantasy," writes Marling, "unhinges the narrative from worldly references . . . and allows us to relax and enjoy the tale."

- As an extension of that freedom, fantasy fiction offers us *endless possibilities*, "the peeling away of expectation and the dissolving of limits."
- *Wonder.*
- *Magic.*
- *Escape* (a mental vacation from our ordinary lives).
- Opportunity to indulge our *imagination*. "Reading fantasy," writes Marling, "gives us license to imagine things that never were and never could have been, and we revel in their impossibility. It allows us to recapture the imaginative games of play we loved as children, which expand our minds and allow us to develop into well-balanced adults."

The Voyage of Maeldune supplies all these elements in great quantity.

The story belongs to a type of Christian Celtic literature called *immram*. These were tales of sea voyages made in round-hulled, skin-covered currachs. The literal translation of the Gaelic word is

"rowing about," and the journeys were never straight
lines from point A to B. Instead, as the phrase "rowing about" suggests, the stories' heroes were willing
to risk losing their way. At one point, Maeldune tells
his men to put down the oars and let God direct
their course with the wind. Maeldune, like the pro-
tagonists of other immram, is willing to surrender
his control and submit to being lost.

Christian monks created the immram stories, but
these sea adventures are an expression of a Christian
perspective that's infused with Paganism (or perhaps
a Pagan perspective infused with Christianity). The
Christian paradise and the Celtic Otherworld cannot
be separated within the tales, and the supernatural
world is full of both angels and enchantment.

Literary historians trace the immram back to
several influences:

- Monastic *mirabilia*. These were written col-
  lections of "wonderful things." They often
  took the form of bestiaries, which were
  compendiums of animals, both real and
  imaginary, with no distinction between the
  two. They expressed the wonder we still feel

today when reading fantasy fiction—and also when encountering the natural world, which is equally wondrous.

- Pre-Christian Celtic voyage tales to magic islands, which fell into a category called *echtrai*, adventures that led the hero into the Otherworld.
- Classical voyage stories such as the Odyssey, the Aeneid, and the story of Jason and the Argonauts. (In fact, some of Maeldune's adventures are very like Odysseus's.)
- Actual sea pilgrimages, know as *peregrinatio pro Christi*, that were a common form of spiritual practice among the early Christian Celts.

Maeldune sets out on his journey because he wants to find the men who killed his father. He is seeking to avenge his father's death—but his voyage turns out to be something else altogether. By the time he returns home, he is a different man, and he has replaced vengeance with forgiveness. Ultimately, his long journey has brought him to a place of grace and reconciliation.

For the ancient Celts, the sea was a liminal place, a place that is betwixt and between the "real" world and the supernatural world. The sea touches both heaven and earth; it stretches out from the known world into the mysterious unknown.

During Maeldune's sea journey, there is no line between the visible and invisible world; he and his men cross back and forth unknowingly as they move from island to island. Between islands are long periods of hunger and thirst—and despair—but eventually they always come to another stopping place, where they find more wonders. Some of their stopping places are idyllic, while others are full of mortal peril; some of the creatures and people they encounter threaten their very lives, while others bless them and help them.

Our experiences are much the same, actually. We too must eventually accept that our lives seldom run a straight A-to-B line from one well-planned goal to the next. Instead, we are "at sea"; we live "not an orderly progression toward a state of grace" but "an unpredictable, arbitrary zig-zag course through the realms of heaven and hell."[2]

We may find, like Maeldune, that when we surrender our attempts to control our lives, when we are willing to risk losing our way, that those are times when we not only encounter new adventures (both painful and joyful) but also make new discoveries. We may experience long stretches of despair, where it seems we are going nowhere, but each time we will eventually find a "stopping place," a time for being restored and refreshed before we venture on.

And ultimately, our life's immram can lead us too to a state of grace.

References

1. Marling, A. E. "Ten Reasons Why We Love the Fantasy Genre," Fantasy Book Critic, February 26, 2013, www.fantasybookcritic. blogspot.com. Accessed May 5, 2015.
2. Hillers, Barbara. "Voyages Between Heaven and Hell: Navigating the Early Irish *Immram* Tales," *Proceedings of the Harvard Celtic Colloquium*, Vol. 13 (1993), pp. 66-81.

1
Maeldune's Beginning

There was a great man of the Eoganacht of the Arans, Ailill of the Edge of Battle his name was. And one time, as he went with the king making war, he fell in with a woman of Kildare, and he forced her; and she bade him to tell her his race and his name. Not long after that, he was killed by robbers in his own place, and they burned his church over him.

The Queen's Foster-Son

At the end of nine months, the woman gave birth to a son, and she gave him the name of Maeldune. After a while, she brought him in secret to the Queen, who was her friend. Maeldune was reared by the Queen, who told everyone that she was his mother. She reared him and the King's three sons in the one cradle and on the one breast and the one knee.

Maeldune was beautiful indeed, and it is likely there was never anyone so beautiful as himself. He grew up to be a young man, fit to use weapons; quiet he was and pleasant in his ways. Even in his play he went beyond all his comrades, in throwing of balls and in running and leaping, and in racing of horses. He took the sway in all these things.

Maeldune Discovers His Heritage

One day now a proud fighting man got to be jealous of Maeldune, and he said in the dint of his anger, "You, whose race and kindred no one knows, and whose father and mother no one knows, to be getting the better of us in every game, whether by land or by water or on the draught board!"

Maeldune was silent when he heard that, for till that time he had thought himself to be a son of the King and of the Queen. He went to the Queen and said to her, "I will not eat and I will not drink till you tell me of my mother and my father."

"Why are you asking after that?" said she. "Do not give heed to the words of the young men. It is I who am your mother," she said, "and the love of no person on earth for a son is greater than my love for you."

"That may be so," he said, "but for all that, it is right for you to make known my own parents to me."

So his foster mother went with him, and gave him into the hand of his mother. Then Maeldune asked his mother to tell him who was his father.

"It is foolishness to ask that," she said, "for if you should know your father, it would not serve you, and you would be no better off, for it is long ago he died."

"It is better for me to know it," said he, "however it may be."

His mother told him the truth then. "Ailill of the Edge of Battle was your father," she said, "of the Eoganacht of Aran."

Then Maeldune went to his father's place and to his own inheritance, and his three foster brothers with him. His kindred welcomed them, and they bade him keep good courage. He and his brothers became champions there.

Maeldune Sets Out to Sea

Some time after that, the graveyard of the Church of Duncluain was full of fighting men that were casting stones. Maeldune's foot was on the burned wall of the church, and he was casting the stone over it. A bitter-tongued man of the people of the church said to Maeldune, "It would be better," he said, "you to avenge the man that was burned there than to be casting stones over his bare burned bones."

"What man was that?" said Maeldune."

"It was Ailill," he said, "your own father."

"Who was it killed him?" said Maeldune.

"It was outlaws of Laighis," he said, "and it was here on this spot he was destroyed."

Then Maeldune was sorrowful, and he threw the stone from him, and took his cloak around him and his fighting-dress. He asked how he might go to Laighis, and those that knew it said he could not go there but by sea only.

So he went into the country of Corcomruadh to ask a charm and good luck of a druid that was there, till he would begin building a boat. The druid told

Maeldune what day he should begin his boat, and the number that should go in it, seventeen men, no more and no less; and he told Maeldune the day he should set out to sea.

Then Maeldune made a boat having three skins on it, and those that were to go with him made ready. German was of them, and Diuran the half-poet. Maeldune set out on the sea the same day the druid had bade him.

When they were gone a little from the land after hoisting the sail, his three foster brothers came to the harbor and called to him to let them go with him.

"Go back home," said Maeldune, "for I cannot bring with me but the number that is here."

"We will go into the sea after you and be drowned if you will not come back to us," they said. Then the three of them threw themselves into the sea and swam out from the land. When Maeldune saw that, he turned back to them that they might not be drowned, and brought them into the currach to him.

2
The Start of His Journey

They were rowing that day till vespers, and the night after till midnight. They rowed on through darkness, looking all the while for land where they might rest.

The Little Bald Islands

At last they found two little bald islands with two houses on them. They heard coming out from the houses the outcries of drunkenness, the cries of the soldiers with their spoils.

"Keep off from me," said the voice of one man, "for I am a better champion than yourself, for it is I killed Ailill of the Edge of Battle, and burned Duncluain on him, and his kindred have done nothing against me. You never did the like of that," he said.

"We have the victory in our hands," said German and Diuran the half-poet. "It is God brought us here and that directed our boat. Let us go and make an attack on those dimnuddies, since God has showed us our enemies."

But while they were saying those words, a great wind came upon them, and they were driven away all that night until morning. Even after daybreak they did not see land or earth, and they did not know where they were going. Then Maeldune said, "Leave the boat quiet without rowing. Wherever God has a mind to bring it, let it go."

They came then into the great ocean that has no ending, and Maeldune said to his foster brothers, "You did this to us, throwing yourselves upon us in the boat against the word of the druid that told us not to let come in the boat but the number we were before you came."

And they had no answer to give, only to stay in silence for a while.

The Island of Ants

Three days and three nights they sailed on, and they did not find land nor ground. On the morning of the third day, they heard a sound from the northeast.

"That is the sound of a wave against the shore," said German.

And when the day was light, they went toward land, and as they were casting lots to know who should go on shore, there came a great swarm of ants, every one of them the size of a foal, down to the strand toward them and into the sea, as if to devour them and their boat. So Maeldune and his men made away and were going over the sea for another three days and three nights, and again they saw neither land nor ground.

The Island of Birds

The morning of the third day, they heard the sound of waves against the strand. With the light of day, they saw an island, big and high with ridges on it, every one of them lower than the other, and trees around it, and great birds on the trees. They were consulting together who would go and search the island, and see what kind were the birds.

"I will go," said Maeldune. So he went and he searched the island, and he found no harmful thing in it. They ate their fill of the birds and brought more of them into the boat.

The Beast That Was Like a Horse

Three days and three nights they were on the sea after that, but on the morning of the fourth day they saw another great island having sandy soil. And when they came to the shore, they saw a beast on it that was like a horse. Legs of a hound he had, with rough sharp nails, and he ran back and forth, as though he were giving a great welcome to them, but he was covetous to devour themselves and their boat.

"He is happy to meet with us," said Maeldune, " but let us go out from the island."

They did that, and when the beast saw them leaving, he went down to the strand, and dug with his sharp nails and pelted sand at them. They feared they would not be able to escape from him, and they used the oars to move faster.

The Demon Riders

They rowed a long way after that, till they saw a great level island before them. This time German chose the lot to go and to search that island, but he feared it was a bad lot.

"The both of us will go," said Diuran the half-poet, taking pity on him, "and you will come with me another time when I am to search out an island."

So the two of them went on the island, great in size and long in length, and they saw a long green lawn, marked with the hooves of horses, and every hoof print was the size of the sail of a ship. They also saw the shells of very large nuts and what was like the leavings of food of many people.

They were in dread of what they saw, and they called to the rest of their people to come and see what they saw. Fear fell on all of them, and they made no delay and went back into their boat. When they had gone out a little from the land, they saw rushing over the sea to the island a great troop. When they reached the green on the island, they began racing their horses. Every horse was faster than the wind, and the air rang with the noise and the shouting.

Maeldune could hear the strokes of the sticks on the horses, and he could hear what the enormous men were saying: "Bring the grey horse!" "Drive the brown horse there beyond!" "Bring the white one!" My horse is the fastest!" "Mine is the best at the leaps!"

And when Maeldune heard the voices, they made away with all their might, for they were sure they were hearing a gathering of demons.

3
God Supplies Food

They went on then through the length of a week in hunger and in thirst, despairing in their hearts that they would ever find land. But Maeldune said to them, "God will bring us to the next stopping place."

A House of Plenty

Then they found an island very big and high, with a large house at the edge of the sea. A door was in the house that faced the level plain of the island, and another door faced the sea, and against that door was a weir of stone with an opening in it. The waves were throwing salmon through the opening into the middle of the house.

The wanderers went into the house then, and they found no one, but what they saw was a very large bed for the head man of the house only, and smaller beds, one for every three of his people, and food for three beside every bed, and a glass vessel with good drink in it beside every bed, and a cup for every vessel. So Maeldune and his companions made a meal off that food and that drink, and they gave thanks to Almighty God that had given them relief from their hunger.

The Apple Stick

When they went from that island, they were went again for a long time hungry and without food, till they found another island with a high cliff around it on every side, and a long narrow wood in it, very long and very narrow. When Maeldune reached the wood, he took a stick in his hand as he passed through it. Three days and three nights the stick was in his hand, and meanwhile the currach was under sail going along by the cliff. And on the third day, he found a cluster of three apples at the end of the stick. And through forty nights he and his men were satisfied with those apples.

The Whirling Beast

They came then to another island with a wall of stone around it. When they came near, a great beast leapt up and went racing about the island, and it seemed to Maeldune to be going faster than the wind. It went then to the high part of the island, where it did the straightening-of-the-body feat, that is, its head was below and its feet above. Then it went back to the way it used to be, and then it turned in its skin, the flesh and the bones going around while the skin outside never moved. After that, the skin outside would turn like a mill, while the flesh and the bones never stirred. It ran like this up and down the island.

Maeldune and his people made away then with all their might. The beast saw them running, and it made for the strand to get hold of them. It began to strike at them, casting stones at them. One of the stones came into the currach and broke through

Maeldune's shield and lodged in the keel of the currach.

The Wicked Horses

It was not long after that they found another high island, and a delightful place with great beasts on it like horses. But the horses were biting each other, each take a piece out of the side of another and tearing away its skin and its flesh. Streams of red blood were breaking out of their sides till the ground was full of it.

So they left that island in such haste as if they were out of their wits. By now, they did not know where in the world they were going, or in what place they would find help or land or country.

The Fiery Pigs

Worn out with hunger and thirst, sad and tired without hope of relief, they came to another island. And in that island there were a great many fruit trees, with large golden apples growing on them. There were beasts like pigs, short and fiery, under those trees. They struck the trees with their hind legs till the apples fell from them, and then the pigs fed on them. The beasts did not show themselves at all from the setting of the sun until the dawn, for they hid in caves of the ground.

Maeldune and his men saw a great many birds out on the waves around about the island; from matins to nones the birds swam away from the island, but from nones to vespers they came back toward the island, reaching it at the going down of the sun. Then the birds stripped off the apples and ate them.

"Let us go into the island where those birds are," said Maeldune, "for it is no harder for us to go there than for the birds."

One of his men went to search the island then, and he called his comrade to him. The ground was hot under their feet, and they could not stop there because of the heat, for it was a fiery country. The beasts hidden within threw out heat into the ground that was over them.

The men brought away a few of the apples with them that first day to be eating in the currach. And with the brightness of the morning sun, the birds went from the island, swimming out to sea. The fiery beasts began putting up their heads out of the caves, and they were eating the apples until the setting of the sun. Once they went back in the caves, the birds came again to eat the apples. And Maeldune went with his people that night, and they gathered up all the apples they found. And those apples drove away both hunger and thirst from them, and they filled their boat with them and put out again to sea.

4
Still Greater Adventures

When the apples were gone, their hunger and thirst
was great, and their mouths and their nostrils were
full of the salt of the sea. At last they got sight of an
island that was no great size, with a castle on it and a
high wall around the castle. The wall was as white as
if it were built of burned lime, or as if it were all one
rock of chalk. It height was great, stretching from
the level of the sea to the clouds. Around the wall
was open land, with many new white houses.

The Little Cat

Maeldune and his men went into the best of the
houses. They saw no one in it but a little cat that
was in the middle of the house, playing about on the
four stone pillars that were there, leaping from one

to another. It looked at the men for a short space, but it did not stop from its play.

After that, the men saw three rows on the wall of the house, from one doorpost to another; the first was a row of brooches of gold and silver with their pins stuck in the wall; the second was a row of collars of gold and of silver, every one of them like the hoops of a vat; and the third row was of great swords with hilts of gold and of silver. The rooms were full of white coverings and shining clothes, and an ox roasted on a fire in the middle of the house beside large vessels filled with good fermented drink.

"Is it for us this is left here?" said Maeldune to the cat.

It merely looked at him for a minute and then began playing again, but Maeldune knew he had been given an answer and that the feast had indeed been left for them. So they ate and they drank and they slept, and they stored up what was left of the food and of the drink.

And when they were ready to leave, Maeldune's third foster brother said to him, "Might I bring away with me one of those necklaces?"

"Do not," said Maeldune, "for you should not think that this house has no guard."

But in spite of that, his foster brother brought a collar with him as he left. And the cat came after him and leapt through him like a fiery arrow. When he was burned till he was but ashes, the cat leapt back again to its pillar.

Maeldune spoke quietly to the cat and calmed it with his words, and then he put the necklace back in its place. He cleared away the ashes from the floor and threw them on the shore of the sea. They went back into the currach, speaking soft of the Lord who had worked with such mystery.

The War of Colors

Early on the morning of the third day after that, they saw another island with a wall of brass down the middle of it, dividing it in two parts. They saw great flocks of sheep on the island, a black flock on the near side of the fence and a white flock on the far side, with a big man separating the flocks. When he threw a white sheep over the near side of the fence to the black sheep, it turned black instantly, and when he threw a black sheep over the fence to the far side, it turned to white in the same way.

Dread fell on the men when they saw that. "It is best for us," said Maeldune, "to throw two sticks into the island, and if they change their color, we will know that our own color would change."

So they threw a stick with black bark on the side where the white sheep were, and it turned to white there and then. Then they threw a peeled white rod on the side where the black sheep were, and it turned to black.

"That is not a good sign," said Maeldune. "Let us not land on the island. It is likely if we had, our own color would have lasted no better than the color of the sticks." So they went back from the island then with a great fear upon them.

The Weighty Calves

On the third day after that, they took notice of another island, large and wide, with a herd of beautiful pigs grazing on it. They killed a young pig, but it was too weighty for them to lift it, so they all came around it and washed it and divided it up, and then they brought it into their boat.

A great mountain was on the island, and Diuran the half-poet and German had a mind to go and view the island from it. When they reached the mountain, they found before them a broad, shallow river. German dipped the handle of his spear in the river, and it instantly was gone where the water had touched, as if fire had burned it to nothing. They did not try to cross the water and went no farther.

They saw then on the other side of the river great hornless oxen lying down and a very big man sitting with them. German banged his spear shaft against his shield to frighten the cattle.

"Why would you frighten these foolish calves?" the big herdsman asked.

"Where are the dams of these calves?" asked German."

"They are on the other side of the mountain," said the man.

The two of them went back then to their comrades, and told them about the enormous cattle. The danger was too great, they agreed, and they all went away.

The Mill of Grudges

After that they found another island, with a great big ugly mill on it. The miller was rough and ugly and withered. When they asked him what mill was this, he said, "It is the mill of the Inver of Trecenand, and everything that is begrudged is ground in it. Half of the corn of this country is ground in this mill," he said.

With that they saw heavy loads past all counting, with men and horses bent under them, coming to the mill and going from it again. But the men got no benefit from the mill's grain, for all that was brought from it was carried away westward.

And when Maeldune and his comrades heard and saw those things, they blessed themselves with the sign of Christ's Cross and went again into their currach.

The Island of Keening

When they went now from the island of the mill, they found a very large island and a great host of people in it. Black they were, both in their bodies and their clothing, and they had bands around their heads, and they were crying and ever-crying.

The two foster brothers of Maeldune drew the lot to land on the island. No sooner did they reach the people that were crying than they were as if one of them, crying and lamenting the same. Then two of them comrades were sent to bring them out from the rest, but those two also bowed themselves down and cried along with the other.

Then Maeldune said, "Let four of you go with your weapons and bring back our men by force. Do not look at the ground or into the air, and put your cloaks over your nostrils and over your mouths, so that you do not breathe the air of the place. And do not take your eyes off your own men."

So the four went as he told them, and they brought back with them the others. And when they were asked what had they seen in that country, all they could say was, "We do not know, only that we could not keep from crying as the others were."

And they made haste to go away from that island.

The Four-Fenced Island

They came after that to another high island that had four fences that divided it into four parts. The first fence was gold, and another was silver, and the third was brazen, and the fourth was crystal. Kings there were in the one division, and queens in another; fighting men in another, and young girls in the last.

One of the young girls went to meet Maeldune and his companions, and they brought them to land. There they gave them food that was like cheese, but whatever taste each one liked best, he would find that the cheese had that taste. And then she gave them drink from a little vessel, so that they slept in drunkenness for three days and three nights. During all that time, the young girl was attending to them, but when they awoke on the third day they were in their boat at sea, and the island and the girl were nowhere to be seen.

And so they went on rowing.

The Woman with the Pail

Then they came to another little island, having a hill on it with a door set into it of brass, and bolts of brass on the door. There was a bridge of crystal to the door, but when they tried to go across the bridge, they fell down backwards. Then they saw a woman coming out from the door, with a pail in her hand, and she lifted a slab of glass out from the bottom of the bridge. There was a well beneath the glass, and she filled the pail from the well and went back again into the dun.

"It is a housekeeper coming for Maeldune," said German.

"Maeldune indeed!" said she and slammed the door shut.

They began then striking at the door, but the sound of their blows on the door was so sweet that it made quieting music that put them to sleep until the next morning.

When they awoke, they saw the same woman coming out of the door with her pail in her hand, and she filled it under the same slab.

"I tell you it is a housekeeper for Maeldune," said German.

"This is what I think of Maeldune!" said she, and she slammed the door shut behind her.

And when they pounded on the door, the same music put them to sleep till the next day.

They were that way through the length of three days and three nights, and on the fourth day, a beautiful woman came to them. A white cloak she had on her, and a band of gold about her golden hair; two sandals of silver on her white-purple feet; a brooch of silver with bosses of gold in her cloak; and a fine silk shirt next to her white skin.

"My welcome to you, Maeldune," said she, and she gave every man of them each his own name. "It is long we have had knowledge and understanding of your coming here," she said. Then she brought them with her into a great house that stood near the sea, and they drew up their currach on the strand.

They saw before them in the house a bed for Maeldune alone, and a bed for every three of his people. She brought them in a basket food that was like curds, and she gave a share to every three, and whatever taste they wished to find on it they found, each what he liked best.

She filled her pail under the same slab and gave them drink. When she knew they had had their fill, she stopped giving it out to them.

"A fitting wife for Maeldune this woman would be," said every one of his people.

She went away from them then, taking her vessel and her pail with her, and Maeldune's people said to him, "Shall we ask her if she would she be your wife?"

"What harm would it do you," said he, "to speak to her?"

So when she came on the morrow, they said to her, "Will you give your friendship to Maeldune and be his wife? And why would you not stop here tonight?" they said.

But she said she did not know what marriage was, and she went from them to her own house.

On the morrow at the same time she came to them; and when they had drunk and were satisfied, they asked her the same questions.

"Tomorrow," she said, "you will get an answer." She went to her own house then, and they went asleep on their beds.

When they awoke they were in their currach, stranded on a rock. The island or the woman or the place where they had been was nowhere to be seen, only the sea around them for as far as they could see.

The Sound Like Psalms

As they went on, they heard in the northeast a great shout and then something that was like the singing of psalms. And that night and the next day until nones, they were rowing forward, seeking was that shout and that singing. At last, they saw an island with high mountains full of birds, black and brown and speckled, and all were calling and crying out very loud. The birdsong was like men and women shouting and singing psalms together.

The Sod from Ireland

They went on a little from that island, until they found another island of no great size with a great many trees in it, and on the trees many birds. And in the island they saw a man clothed with his own hair, and they asked who was he and what was his race.

"It is of the men of Ireland I am," he said. "I went on my pilgrimage in a little currach, and my currach split under me when I was gone a little way from land. And the Lord settled down the sod from my home in this place," he said, "and it is God who adds a foot to its breadth every year from that time to this, and a tree every year to grow from it. And the birds you see in the trees," he said, "are the souls of my children and my kindred, women and men, who are there waiting for the day of judgment. Half a cake, and a bit of a fish, and a drink from the well, God has given me, and that comes to me every day," he said, "through the service of angels. And besides that," he said, "at the hour of nones, another half a cake and a bit of fish come to every man and to every woman over there, and a drink out of the well that is enough for everyone."

And when their three nights of feasting were at an end on the island, they bade the man farewell, and he said to them, "You will all reach to your own country," he said, "but one man only will not go home."

The Well of Nourishment

The third day after that they found another island with a golden wall around it, and the middle of it was white as feathers. A man was inside the wall, clothed only in the hair of his own body. They asked him then what nourishment he used.

"I will tell you the truth," he said, "there is a well in this island, and on a Friday and on a Wednesday, whey or water flows out from it, and on Sunday and on the feasts of martyrs, it is good milk that flows out. But on the feasts of the apostles and of Mary and John Baptist and on the high times of the year, it is beer and wine that it flows from it."

At nones then there came to every man of them a cake and a bit of a fish, and they drank their fill of what came to them from the well. And it cast them into a sleep of such deep sleeping that it carried them until the morrow.

At the end of three nights. the clerk bade them to go on. So they went on their way and bade him farewell.

The Smiths at the Forge

And when they had been a long time on the waves, they saw an island a long way off. As they came near it, they heard the noise of smiths striking iron on the anvil with hammers, like the striking of three or four. And when they came nearer yet, they heard one man say to another, "Are they near us?"

"They are near us," said the other.

"Who do you say are coming?" said another man.

"Little lads they seem to be in a little trough beyond," said the first.

When Maeldune heard what the smiths were saying, he said, "Let us go back and let us not turn the boat but let her stern be foremost, so they will not know us to be making away from them."

They rowed away then, with the stern of the boat foremost. And they heard the same man said to the other in the forge, "Are they near the harbor now?"

"They are not stirring," said the man who was looking out. "They do not come here and they do not go there," he said.

Soon the first man asked, "What are they doing now?"

"I think," said the man who was looking out, "that they are making away, for they are farther from the port now than they were a while ago."

Then the smith came out from the forge with a great lump of red-hot iron in the tongs in his hand, and he threw it after the boat into the sea. The whole of the sea boiled up, but the iron did not reach to the currach, for the men rowed with their whole strength quickly and with no delay into the great ocean.

The Very Clear Sea

They went on after that till they came to a sea that was like glass, and so clear it was that the gravel and the sand of the sea could be seen through it. They saw no beasts or no monsters at all among the rocks, but only the clean gravel and the grey sand. And through a great part of the day they spent sailing over that sea, and it was very grand it was and beautiful.

The Sea Like a Mist

Then they put out into another sea that was like a cloud, and it seemed to them that it could not support themselves or the currach. But after that they saw below them walled hills and a beautiful country.

A great terrible beast was there in a tree; and a herd of cattle were around about the tree, with a man beside it who had a shield and spear and sword. When he saw the great beast that was in the tree, he instantly ran away. The beast stretched out its neck and stooped his head and grabbed the back of the ox that was biggest of the herd. Then he dragged it into the tree and ate it in the wink of an eye.

The flocks and the herdsmen ran away, and Maeldune and his people were filled with dread. The feared they would never cross that sea without slipping down through it, for it was thin as a mist. But in the end, they got away from it, though there was great danger.

The Pelting with Nuts

After that, they found another island. The sea rose up around it, making great cliffs of water on every side. When the people of that country saw them, they began screaming at them, saying, "It is them! It is them!" till they were out of breath.

Then Maeldune and his men saw a great many people, great herds of cattle and horses, and a great many flocks of sheep. A woman began pelting them with enormous nuts.

The nuts floated on the waves about them, and they gathered up a good share of them to bring away with them. At last, when they had rowed away from the island, they heard the screams come to an end.

"Where are they now?" they heard a man saying.

"They are gone away," said another.

"They are not," said another.

Maeldune and his people talked among themselves and decided that the people of that island had a prophecy that some person would come who would destroy their country and drive them away out of it. That was the only sense they could make out of how the people had acted.

The Salmon Stream

They went on then to another island, where they saw a strange thing: a great stream rose up out of the strand that went like a rainbow over the whole island until it came down on the strand on the other side. They found they could go under the stream without getting any wet.

When they pierced the stream above, very large salmon fell from the stream above onto the ground. The whole island was full of the smell of salmon.

From the evening of Sunday until the full light of Monday, that stream did not move. It stopped in its silence where it was in the sea. Maeldune and his companions brought together the biggest of the salmon into one place, and they filled their currach with them. Then they went on their way, away over the ocean.

The Silver-Meshed Net

They went on then till they found a great silver pillar; four sides it had and the width of each of the sides was two strokes of an oar. Not one sod of earth was around it, only the endless ocean. They could not see how deep it went, and they could not see its top, so tall was it. A silver net spread out from the top of the pillar a long way on every side. The currach went under sail through the net's mesh.

Then Diuran tried to rip the mesh with his spear.

"Do not destroy the net," said Maeldune, "for we are looking at the work of great men."

"It is for the praise of God's name I am doing it," said Diuran, "so that my story will be better believed. I will give this net's mesh to the altar of Ardmacha if I get back to Ireland."

They heard then a voice from the top of the pillar, very loud and clear, but they did not know in what strange language it was speaking, nor could they understand a word it said.

The Door Under Locks

They saw then another island that had a single foot supporting it. They rowed around the island, looking for a way to come on shore, but they found none. Then they saw down at the bottom of the foot a closed door with locks, and they realized that this was the only way the island could be entered. They saw a plough at the height of the island, but they spoke with no one and no one spoke with them, so they went on their way.

5
Maeldune Is Enamored

They came after that to an island with a great plain on it that was smooth and grassy. A great hill stood near the sea, high and strong, with a large house on it. The house had good beds, and seventeen girls were in it making a bath ready.

They landed then on that island and sat down on the grass in front of the gate. Maeldune said, "I am sure it is for us that bath is being made ready."

The Queen

At the hour of nones, they saw a woman on a horse of victory coming to them. A well-ornamented cloth she had under her, and a blue embroidered hood on her head; a fringed crimson cloak, gloves worked with gold on her hands, and beautiful sandals on her feet. As she got down, one of the young girls came out and took her horse, and she went in to the house and into the bath. Before long a girl came to them and said, "Your coming is welcome. And come now inside. It is the queen who invites you."

So they went inside and they all washed in the bath. Afterward, the queen sat on one side of the house with her seventeen girls around her, and Maeldune sat on the other side, but near the queen, with his seventeen men around him Then a dish of good food was brought to Maeldune, and a vessel of glass that was full of good drink, and a dish and a vessel for every three of his people.

They spent the night there in the seventeen rooms of the house, and Maeldune slept with the queen. And when they rose up in the morning, the queen said, "If you will stay here, no age will fall on you beyond the age you are at now, and you will have lasting life for ever. What you got last night you will get forever without any labor. Give up this wandering from island to island of the sea."

"Tell us," said Maeldune "how are you here?"

"It is not hard to answer," she said. "There was a good man in this place, the king of the island, and I bore him seventeen daughters. And then he died and left no man to inherit after him, and I myself took the kingship of the island. And every day," she said, "I go into the great plain there beyond to give out judgments and to settle the disputes of the people. I will go there now."

"Why would you go from us today?" said Maeldune.

"Unless I go," she said, "what happened to us last night will not happen to us again. But you may stay in the house while I am gone," she said, "and there is no need for you to work. I will go judge the people, and you need do nothing."

A Long Stay

They stayed on that island through the three months of the winter, but it seemed to them they had been there three years.

"It is long we are here," said a man of Maeldune's people to him finally. "Why do we not go back to our own country?"

"What you are saying is not right," said Maeldune, "for we will not find in our own country any better thing than what we are getting here."

His people began to murmur greatly against him then, saying, "He has great love for the queen. Let him stop with her if he has a mind," they said, "and we will go to our own country."

"No," said Maeldune, "I will not stay here without you."

The Ball of Thread

One day now the queen went to the judging where she went every day, and no sooner was she gone than they went into their currach. But she came on her horse and she threw a ball of thread after them, and Maeldune caught it. It wrapped around his hand, and with it she drew back the boat to the harbor and to herself.

Then they stayed with her for another three months. At last, they made to leave again, but she brought them back with a thread the same as she did before. Three times this happened, and at last they consulted among themselves then.

"It is certain," they said, "that Maeldune has great love for this woman. That is why he catches the ball of thread, and that is why it wraps around his hand, and that is why we are brought back to the island each time."

"Let some other one take the thread next time," said Maeldune, "and if it wraps around his hand, let the hand be cut off him."

So they went on then to their boat, and just as before, the queen came and threw the ball after them. This time another man in the currach caught it. When it wrapped around his hand, Diuran struck off the hand, and it fell and the thread with it into the sea. And when the queen saw that she began to cry and to call out till the whole island was one loud cry and one lament. And in that way they at last made their escape from her.

6
Wonder upon Wonder

For a long while after that they were driven about on the waves, and yet again despair filled their hearts. But Maeldune told them again to trust in God who was leading them.

The Wonderful Trees

At last, they found an island having trees on it like willow or hazel, with large wonderful berries on the trees. So they stripped a little tree and they cast lots who should try the berries. The lot fell upon Maeldune.

He squeezed some of the berries into a vessel and drank, and it put him into a deep sleep from that hour to the same hour on the morrow. They did not know if he were alive or dead, with the red foam around his lips, till he awoke on the morrow. He said to them then, "Go ahead and gather this fruit, for it has great good in it."

So they gathered all there was of it, and they squeezed it and filled the vessels they had with them. They mixed water with the juice to lessen the sleep of its drunkenness. And after that was done, they rowed away from that island.

The Bird That Got Back Its Youth

After that they stopped at another large island, the one side of it a wood with yews and great oaks on it, and the other side a plain with a little lake and great flocks of sheep on the plain. They saw a little church, and when they went to the church, they found an old grey priest, clothed entirely in his own hair.

"Eat now your fill of the sheep," he said, "but do not use more than is enough."

So they stopped there for a while, and fed upon the flesh of the sheep. One day, as they were looking out from the island, they saw a cloud coming toward them from the southwest. After a while, they could see it to be a bird, for they could see its wings moving. Then it came to the island and lit upon a hill near the lake, and they feared it would carry them in its claws out to sea. It had with it a branch of a great tree, and the branch was bigger than one of the great oaks there. The branch had twigs on it and plenty of heavy fruit, and the top of it was full of fresh leaves.

Maeldune and his men hid, watching to see what the bird would do. It seemed to be tired, for it stayed quiet for a while, and then it began to eat the fruit of the tree. So Maeldune went to the edge of the hill where the bird was, to see if it would do him any harm. It did not meddle with him, so then all his people followed him.

"Let one of us go," said Maeldune, "and gather some of the fruit that is by the bird."

So one man went then and gathered a share of the berries. The bird made no complaint and did not look at him or make any stir at all. And then all of them went behind the bird, carrying their shields with them, and it did them no harm.

Toward the hour of nones, they saw two eagles in the southwest, in the same quarter the great bird had come from. They perched in front of the great bird, where they stood quiet for a good while. When they were rested, they began to take off the lice that were on the great bird's jaws and its eyes and its ears. They went on doing that till vespers, and then the three of them began to eat the berries of the branch.

Then from the morning of the morrow till the middle of the day, they were picking at the great bird in the same way, and stripping the old feathers from it and the scabs. But when midday came, they began to strip the berries from the branch, and they were crushing them against the stones with their beaks and throwing them into the lake till the foam of it turned to red. After that, the great bird went into the lake and washed himself there till toward the end of the day. Then he went out of the lake and perched in another place on the same hill, so that the lice that were picked out of him would not settle on him again.

And on the morning of the morrow, the same two eagles dressed and smoothed the feathers of the great bird as if they were using a comb, and they kept at that until midday, and then they went away the same way as they had come. But the great bird stared after them, shaking out his wings and his feathers till the end of the third day. And at the hour of tierce on the third day, he rose up and flew three times round the island. Then he perched for a little rest on the same hill, and after that he rose and went away far off toward the southwest where he came from, his flight far swifter and stronger than when he came.

They all knew then that he had been renewed from old age to youth, after the word of the prophet that said, "Thy youth shall be renewed like the eagle's.

Diuran said, seeing that great wonder, "Let us go into the lake to renew ourselves the same as the bird."

"Do not," said another, "for the bird has left his poison in it."

"No, you are wrong," said Diuran, "and I will go into the water first myself." He went in then and bathed himself there and put his lips into the water and drank sups of it. From that day on, his eyes were young and strong, and they were so for as long as he was living. He never lost a tooth or a hair from his head, and he was never sick or sorry from that day on.

They bade farewell then to the old man dressed in his hair, and they took a share of the sheep with them for provision. Then they put out their boat and went on their way over the ocean.

The Laughing People

Then they found another island with wide level plain on it. A great crowd of people were on that plain, playing and laughing without end. Maeldune and his men cast lots then who would go and search out the island, and the lot fell on the head of the third of Maeldune's foster brothers.

No sooner did he land on the island than he began to play and to laugh along with the people that were on it, as if he had been one of them from the beginning. His comrades stopped there for a long time waiting for him, but he never came back to them; so they left him there.

The Fire-Walled Island

After that they saw another island that was no great size, with a fiery wall around it that moved around and around the island in a whirling circle. There was an open door in the side of the wall, but it was constantly turning around. Whenever the door would come opposite them, Maeldune and his companions could see the whole island through it, and all that was on it. They saw all the people who lived there, beautiful and wearing embroidered clothes, with golden vessels in their hands, feasting. And they could hear the ale-music the people were making. They stayed there for a long time, looking through the door whenever it came around. They thought it was delightful.

7
The Greedy Man

They were not long gone from that island when they saw far off among the waves a shape like a white bird, so they turned the prow of the boat southward, till they could see what was it. When they came near, they saw it was a man, clothed only with the white hair of his body. He was throwing himself and stretching himself upon a wide rock.

When they reached him, they asked a blessing of him, and then they asked where he had come from to that rock.

His Story

"It is from Toraig I am come surely," he said, "and it is in Toraig I was reared. And this is what happened: I was a cook but it is a bad cook I was, for

I used to be selling for means and for treasures for myself the food of the church where I was, so that my house grew to be full of quilts and of pillows and of clothes, both linen and woolen, of every color, and of pails of brass and of silver, and brooches of silver having pins of gold. There was nothing wanting in my house of all that people most desire, both of golden books and of bags for books ornamented with silver and gold. And I used to dig under the houses of the church, and I brought many treasures from them. Great was my pride and my boasting.

"One day, now, I was bade to dig a grave for the body of a countryman who had been brought to the island. As I was at the grave, I heard a voice coming up under my feet. 'Do not dig in that place,' it said. 'Do not put the body of a sinner upon me, a holy, religious person.'

"'I will put it between myself and God,' said I in the greatness of my pride.

"'If that is so,' said the voice, 'your mouth shall perish on the third day from this, and it is in hell you will be, but your body will not stay here.'

"'What will you give me if I do not lay the body upon you?' said I.

"'Lasting life with God,' said he.

"'How can I know that?' said I.

"'That will not be hard,' said he. 'The grave you are digging now will be full of sand, and it will be showed to you by the fact that you cannot lay the body upon me however much you may try.' Those words were hardly said when the grave was full of sand. So after that I buried the body in another place.

"One time then I put out a new currach, having red hide over it, on the sea. And I went into the currach and I was well pleased at everything I saw. I left nothing in my house, small or great. I brought it all with me, vats and drinking vessels and horns. And while I was looking at the sea, at first it was calm, but then great winds came upon me and brought me away in to the sea till I did not see land nor ground. And then my currach stayed still, and from then on it did not stir from the place where it was.

"As I was looking about me on every side I saw to my right hand the man who had spoken from the grave, sitting on the waves. He said to me, 'Where are you going?'

"'I like well,' I said, 'the view I have over the sea.'

"'You would not like it well,' he said, 'if you could see the troop that is all around you.'

'What troop is that?' asked I.

"'There is nothing so far as your sight reaches over the sea and up to the clouds,' he said, 'but one troop of demons all around you.'

"'But why?' asked I.

"'By reason of your covetousness,' said he, 'and your vanity and your pride and your theft and your other bad deeds. And do you know why it is your boat has stopped where it is?'

"'I do not know that indeed,' I said.

"'The currach will not go out of the place where it is,' he said, 'until such time as you will do my bidding.'

"'Maybe I will not put up with that,' said I.

"'You will give in to the pains of hell unless you give in to my will,' said he. He came toward me then, and laid his hand upon me and I said I would do his bidding. 'Throw out into the sea,' he said, 'all the riches you have stored in the boat.'

'It would be a pity,' said I, 'that all should go to loss.'

"'It will not go to loss,' said he. 'There is one who will profit by it.'

I threw out then into the sea all that was in the boat but one small wooden cup.

"'Go on now,' he said, 'and wherever your currach stops, stay in that place.' And he gave me provisions then, a cupful of whey water and seven cakes.

"So I went on then," said the old man, "where my currach and the wind brought me for I had let my oars and the rudder go. And as I was moving on the waves, I was cast upon this rock. At first I was in doubt if the boat had stopped, for I saw neither land nor ground. And I brought to mind then what had been said to me, to stay in the place where my boat would stop. So I raised myself up and I saw I was on a little rock with the waves laughing about it. Then I set my foot on the little rock, and the rock lifted me up and the waves went from it.

"Seven years I was here," he said, "with only the seven cakes to eat, and at the end of that time the cakes failed me. Then I had only the cup of whey water. After I had fasted three days, at the hour of nones an otter brought a salmon to me out of the sea. I said to myself in my mind I would never be satisfied to eat the salmon raw, and I put it out again into the sea. Then I was fasting through the length of another three days. And at the third none I saw the otter bringing the salmon to me again out of the sea; and another otter brought kindled wood and put it down and blew it with his breath so that the fire blazed up. So I roasted the salmon, and for another seven years I lived that way.

"A salmon would come to me every day," he said, "and with it fire wood, and the rock was increasing until now it is large. And at the end of the seven years," he said, "my salmon was not given to me, and I was fasting through another three days. And at the third none half a wheaten cake and a bit of a fish washed up to me. Then my cup of whey water went from me, and there came to me a cup of the same size that was full of good drink. It is here on the rock now, and it is full every day. Now neither wind nor wet nor heat nor cold vexes me in this place.

"And that is my story for you," said the old man.

CDaeldune Receives Wise Advice

When the hour of none was come, the half of a cake and a bit of a fish came for every man of them. They drank their full of good drink from the cup that was on the rock with the old man.

The old man said to them then, "You will all reach your country. You will find the man who killed your father, Maeldune, but do not kill him. Instead, give forgiveness since God has saved you from many great dangers, and you yourselves are deserving of death the same as himself."

They bade farewell then to the old man, and they went on as they had before. And as to the commandment he had given, it is well Maeldune kept it in mind and obeyed it afterwards.

8
Maeldune's Homecoming

After they were gone from old man, they came to an island that had a great many cattle, oxen, cows, and sheep, but there were no houses on it. They ate the flesh of the sheep, and as they ate, one of them looked up at the sky

The Bird from Ireland

A bird was flying overhead, and the man said, "That bird is like the birds of Ireland."

"That is true indeed," said some of the rest.

"Keep watch on it," said Maeldune, "and see what way it will go."

They saw then the bird flying from them to the southeast, and they rowed after it in that direction and they went on rowing until vespers.

Maeldune Is Welcomed Home

At the fall of night, they came in sight of land that was like the land of Ireland. They rowed toward it, and they found a small island. It was from that very island the wind had brought them into the ocean the time they first put to sea.

They drew their boat on shore then, and they went to the castle that was on the island. The people there were at their supper at that time, and they heard some of them saying, "It will be well for us if we never see Maeldune again."

"Maeldune was drowned," said another man.

"If he should come in now," said another, "what would we do?"

"That is not hard to answer," said the man of the house. "There would be a great welcome for him if he should come, for it is a long time he has been under great hardship."

With that Maeldune struck the hand-wood against the door.

"Who is there?" said the doorkeeper.

"Maeldune is here."

"Open the door then," said the man of the house, "for your coming is welcome."

They came into the house then, and a great welcome was laid before them and new clothing was given to them. Then they bore witness to all the wonders God had showed to them. They told their journey from beginning to end, and all the troubles and dangers they had found by land and sea. It was like the words of the holy hymn that said, *Haec olim meminisse juvabit*—"One day we will will look back on this and smile."

And then Maeldune went to his own district, and Diuran the half-poet took the five half ounces of silver he had taken from the net and laid them on the altar of Ardmacha in joy and in triumph at the miracles and great wonders God had done for them.

Aedh Finn, now chief storyteller of Ireland, put down this story the way it is here. He did it for gladdening the mind and for the people of Ireland who would come after him.

PART VI

STORIES OF
THE CELTIC SAINTS

The faith of the early Christian Celts—while passionately in love with the Threefold Christian God, especially the Son of the High King—was also steeped in the flavor of the pagan beliefs it expanded and enriched but never totally replaced. The Otherworld was just next door, so miracles and wonders were to be expected. Creativity and the arts were valued and practiced with devotion. Jesus might be found in any person, and so his Celtic followers felt challenged to see and love him in all his guises. This was not always easy to do, however, even for the mystical Celts, as we see in the story of the seventh-century Saint Moling.

The stories of Saint Ciaran date back to the sixth century. There were two Celtic saints named Ciaran, but the one whose story is included here is Ciaran of Saigir, who was born in the fifth century. Before he was conceived, his mother dreamed a star fell into her mouth. When she told her dream to the

Druids—the wise men of Celtic culture—they told her that she would bear a son whose fame and virtue would be known as far as the world's end. When her son grew up, he became a holy man who dressed in animal skins and lived in the woods. Like a Celtic John the Baptist, he is said to have come before Saint Patrick (just as John came before Christ) and prepared the way for Patrick's work.

The Celts saw the natural world as both an intimate friend and a beloved revelation of the Divine. They cherished and respected animals. Saint Ciaran's first students were the forest animals; Saint Colman had a mouse for a friend. We may doubt that the mouse made sure his human friend kept the Holy Hours, and we may find it hard to believe the story where bees build an altar and celebrate mass—but what these stories reveal is the Celts' sense that animals were humans' equals before God. They were as capable of receiving and expressing Divine love as any person, which for the Celtic saints meant that they were to be treated with compassion and friendship. Humans and animals were so intimately connected that shapeshifting was considered a real possibility, as we see in the story of Tuan. These beliefs were part of the Christian Celts' pagan heritage, and beliefs like this continued to form the shape through which they saw the world. From their perspective, Christianity had fulfilled rather than erased the reality they had known before they followed Christ.

The theology behind these beliefs is spelled out even more clearly in the stories of the Ever-New Tongue. This text, written in the ninth or tenth centuries, remained popular through the Middle Ages and became part of Celtic folk traditions as well. It relates how Christ's resurrection brought redemption to the whole of creation, not just to humankind: "When Christ arose, all the world arose with him, for all the elements dwelled in the Body of Jesus." This perspective on the natural world was far different from the exploitive one favored by much of the Western world's religion.

The Celts saw time as something fluid; their saints could easily step out of its stream both backward and forward. Nor did death put an end to their work on earth; even in the twenty-first century, many Celts believe that Ciaran and Colman and Moling (not to mention Patrick and Brigit) are still lingering around their holy wells and shrines, eager to lend a helping hand to those in trouble.

For many of us, the world of the ancient Celts may seem misty and faraway, obscured by legend and fairytales. The stories here reveal some of the reality of that world. Whether or not we believe that the ancient saints are still present among us, we can learn much from them. Their world can enrich our own lives today.

1

Blessed Ciaran

The first of the saints to be born in Ireland of the saints was Ciaran, who was of the blood of the nobles of Leinster. And the first of the wonders he did was in the island of Cleire, and he but a young child at the time.

There came a hawk in the air over his head, and it stooped down before him and took up a little bird that was sitting on a nest. Pity for the little bird came over Ciaran, and he was in pain from it. Then the hawk turned back and left the bird, half dead and trembling. Ciaran spoke to it and bade it to rise up. And it rose and went up safe and well to its nest, by the grace of God.

It was Patrick who bade Ciaran after that to go to the Well of Uaran, the boundary where the north meets with the south in the middle part of Ireland.

"And bring my little bell with you," Patrick said, "and it will be without speaking till you come to the Well."

So Ciaran did that, and when he reached to the Well of Uaran (for God brought him there), the little bell spoke out at that moment in a bright, clear voice. And Ciaran settled himself there, and he all alone, with great woods all around the place. He began to make a little cell for himself.

One time, as he was sitting under the shadow of a tree, a wild boar rose up on the other side of the tree. When it saw Ciaran, it ran from him—and then it turned back again, as a quiet servant to him, being made gentle by God. That boar was the first scholar and the first monk Ciaran had. It went into the wood and plucked rods and thatch between its teeth as if to help Ciaran with his building.

More wild creatures came to Ciaran from out of the places where they were: a fox and a badger and a wolf and a doe. They were tame with him and listened to his teaching the same as brothers, and they did all he bade them to do.

But one day the fox, who was greedy and cunning and full of malice, found Ciaran's shoes and he stole them. He went away, shunning the rest of the company, to his own old den, for he had a mind to eat the brogues. But Ciaran saw in his mind what had happened, and he sent another monk from the monks of his family—the badger—to bring back the fox to the place where they all were. So the badger went to the cave where the fox was and found him. The fox was eating the thongs and the ears of the shoes, but the badger made him come back with him to Ciaran. They came to Ciaran in the evening, bringing the brogues with them.

And Ciaran said to the fox, "O brother, why did you do this robbery that was not right for a monk to do? And there was no need for you to do it," he said, "for we all have food and water in common, that we harm no one with what we eat. But if your nature told you it was better for you to eat flesh, God would have made it for you from the bark of those trees. For God supplies when we cease hurting others to get what we need."

Then the fox asked Ciaran to forgive him and to put a penance on him; and Ciaran did. From then on, the fox never ate unless he had leave from Ciaran. From that time on, he was as honest as the rest.

His Kindness Is Living Yet

Not long ago, a poor woman of Aidne who did spinning for the neighbors brought her little son who was lame to the blessed well of Ciaran. And when she and her son looked in the well, they saw a little fish tossing and leaping and the water bubbling up. The woman said, "I have been coming here for many years, but I never saw that fish until now." And from that time the lameness went from the little lad.

And there was a poor woman in Connacht who fretted greatly because she was told that her son who was in America had lost his leg under a train. She worried that maybe she had not heard all the truth, that the neighbors might be hiding from her that he was dead. So she went to the well of blessed Ciaran and she kneeled down on the stones. Then she prayed three times to God and to the saint to give her a sign. After the third time, a little fish rose up and went swimming and stirring itself at the top of the water as if to show itself. She saw that a piece had been taken out of it, and that it was lively all the same. And sure enough, her son got well and is living in America yet. And many others who have someone belonging to them across the ocean will go and ask for a sign at that well, and it will be given to them the same as it was to her.

2
Saint Moling

Faelan the Fair, son of Feradach, owned many lands in Luachair, and he and his wife lacked nothing. Now his wife had with her a sister by the name of Emnait, and Faelan set his heart on her and won her love. When she became great with child, fear and dread seized her, on account of her sister, and she fled and traveled by night back to her home. It was the midst of winter when the snow was so deep that it reached men's shoulders, and she gave birth to her babe in the snow, in the dark and the cold. The boy was sweet and beautiful, sweet and shining. A company of angels arrived and melted the snow around the child for thirty feet on every side.

Emnait thought to kill the child because of her great fear and shame, but a white dove spread its wings around the baby, keeping him warm and protecting him throughout the night. The next morning, Collanach, a monk and sage, took them in and baptized the child and gave him the name Tairchell. Collanach taught the boy, and he learned much, and he was taught too by an angel, by the Angel Victor himself.

When Tairchell had completed sixteen years, he set out to journey on a circuit of Luachair, and as he completed his circuit, he came upon a misshapen, black, and ugly monster on the path ahead, a dark and singed goblin. The Evil Specter had with him his wife, his servant, his hound, and his nine followers, and each were both human and goblin.

Said the Specter to his household, "Since I took to murder and marauding, I never wished to protect any soul save for him yonder. Let me go and speak with him."

So the Specter approached Tairchell and spoke with him and warned him that he and his followers would destroy him. But Tairchell convinced the Specter that they could not do so, for the ash staff he carried had promised to destroy any who attacked him. "Grant me instead a boon," said Tairchell then.

"What boon is that?" asked they.

"Let me have three steps as long as a pilgrim's passage toward the King of heaven and earth. And then for my sheer folly, give me three leaps."

"Let it be granted to you," said the hag, "but we will still overtake you, for we ourselves are swift as wild deer, and our hound is as swift as the wind."

Then Tairchell leapt his first step, and it was no farther than a crow could hop. But his second leap took him away from them so far that the specters saw him no longer, and they knew not whether he was on earth or had gone to heaven. And on the third leap, he landed on the wall around the church where he had been raised.

"He has gone yonder," said the hag, and she and the rest of them ran, both hound and human, so that their storm and outcry could be heard for a thousand paces.

The hounds and the folk of the village came out and gathered around Tairchell to protect him, and Tairchell leapt from the wall and went into the church, to his place of prayer, where he began chanting the psalms with the others.

But Collanach, his foster father, saw the glow of anger upon him and the radiance of the Godhead in his countenance, and he said to Tairchell, "What is the rage of wrath I see on your face?"

Tairchell related to him all that had happened, and when he had finished, Collanach said to him, "You are the prophesied one, whom the Angel Victor foretold. And because of your leaps, you will be called now Moling." ("Ling" meaning leap.)

Moling then served the Lord and wrought miracles and marvels. He brought the dead to life; he healed the blind and lepers and cripples and sufferers from every disease. He preached God's word to everyone. An angel of God often was comforting him and tending him, persuading him to every good thing and hindering every evil.

Moling's Guest

As Moling was praying in his church one time, he saw a young man coming into the house. A comely shape he had and purple clothing.

"Good be with you, Clerk," he said.

"Amen," said Moling.

"Why do you give me no blessing?" said the young man.

"Who are you?" said Moling.

"I am Jesus Christ the Son of God."

"That is not so," said Moling. "In the time Christ used to come to us and to be talking with the servants of God, He was not in purple or like a king. He came in the shape of the miserable, the poor, and the lepers."

"If you do not believe me," said the young man, "who do you think I am?"

"In my opinion," said Moling, "you are the devil, coming to do me harm."

"Your unbelief is what is harmful to you," said the young man, "and not myself."

"Well," said Moling, "here is your successor, the Gospel of Christ," and with that, he raised up the book.

"Do not raise that up, Clerk," said the young man then, "for what if I am after all what you say, a man full of trouble?"

"Why have you come?" said Moling.

"To ask a blessing of you," said the young man.

"I will not give it," said Moling, "for no blessing would make you better. What good would it be to you?"

"O Clerk," said the young man, "it would as if you went into a vat of honey with your clothing on, and bathed yourself in honey—the smell of honey would be all around you when you came out, unless you washed your clothing. That is how your blessing would be to me."

"I will not give it to you," said Molling, "for I do not believe it is your true desire."

"Well," the young man said, "give me then the full measure of a curse."

"What good will that do you?" said Moling.

"The answer is not hard, Clerk. If your mouth should curse me, its hurt and its poison would be on your lips."

"Go," said Moling, "you are worthy of no blessing."

"Well, then," said the young man, "it would be best for me to earn it. How can I do that?"

"By serving God," said Moling.

"My grief," he said, "I cannot do that for I know not how."

"By fasting then."

"I am fasting since the beginning of the world," he said, "and I am none the better for it."

"Bow your knees," said Moling."

"I cannot do that for my knees are turned backwards."

"Go out from my house," said Moling, "for I cannot save you."

But then, before the stranger went, he sang these words:

He is clean gold, he is Heaven about the sun,
he is a silver vessel having wine in it;
he is an angel, he is the wisdom of saints;
everyone is doing the will of the King.

He is a bird with a trap closing about him;
he is a broken ship in great danger;
he is an empty vessel, he is a withered tree;
he that is not doing the will of the King.

He is a sweet-smelling branch with its blossoms;
he is a vessel that is full of honey;

he is a shining stone of good luck;
he who does the will of the Son of God of heaven.

He is a blind nut without profit;
he is ill-smelling rottenness,
he is a withered tree;
he is a wild apple branch without blossom;
he that is not doing the will of the King.

He is the Son of God of Heaven,
he is a bright sun with summer about it;
he is the image of the God of Heaven;
he is a vessel of clear glass.
He is a racehorse over a smooth plain,
a chariot that wins the victory with golden bridles.
He is a sun that warms high heaven;
the king to whom the great King is thankful;
he is a church, joyful, noble;
he is a shrine having gold about it.

He is an altar having wine poured upon it;
having many quires singing around;
he is a clean chalice with ale in it;

he is bronze, white, shining; he is gold.
Everyone and everyone is doing the will of the King.

And Moling sorrowed then that he had withheld his blessing.

Moling Goes to His Resting Place

Moling was a poet, a prophet, a knower, a teacher, a sage, a psalmist, a priest, a bishop, and a soul friend. In the eighty-second year of his life, with quiring of the household of heaven and with prayer of the household of earth, after fasting and almsgiving and prayer and fulfillment of every good thing, Moling went to his resting place with the angels.

3
Saint Colman

When Rhinagh of the race of Dathi was with child by Duach, the King of Connacht of that time heard that the son she would bear would be greater than his own sons. When he heard that, he told his people to put an end to Rhinagh before the child could be born.

They took her and tied a heavy stone about her neck and threw her into the deep part of the river, where it rises inside Coole. But by the help of God, the stone that was put about her neck did not sink but went floating upon the water, and she came to the shore and was saved from drowning. And that stone is to be seen yet, with the mark of the rope that was put around it.

A Blind Man and a Lame Man

Just at that time, a blind man had a dream in the north about a well beside a certain ash tree at Kiltartan, and he was told in the dream he would get his sight if he bathed in the water of that well. And a lame man had a dream about the same well, that he would find healing in it for his lameness. The two men set out together, the lame man carrying the man that had lost his sight, till they came to the tree they had dreamed about.

But all the field was dry, and there was no sign of water except a bunch of green rushes beside the ash tree. Then the lame man saw a light shining out from among the rushes, and when they came near, they heard the cry of a child. There by the tree was the little baby that was afterwards Saint Colman.

And they took him up and they said, "If we had water we would baptize him." With that, they pulled up a root of the rushes, and a well sprang up and they baptized him; and that well is there to this day.

The water splashed upon them as it was springing up, and the lame man was cured of his lameness, and the blind man got his sight. And many that would have their blindness cured go and sleep beside that well even still.

Colman's Mouse

Colman was a great saint afterwards, and his name is in every place. Seven years he lived in Burren in a cleft of the mountains, with no one in it but himself and a mouse. He kept the mouse as companion and friend, and it would awaken him when he was asleep when the time came for him to mind the Hours. Mouse and man praised the Lord together.

The Little Lad in the Well

There was a boy fell into the blessed well of Saint Colman that is near the seven churches at Kilmacdu-agh, a little lad he was at the time, wearing a little red petticoat and a little white jacket. And when some of the people of the house went to draw water, they looked down in the well and saw him standing up in the water. They got him out and brought him in to the fire and he was none the worse. And he said it was a little grey man who came to him in the well and put his hand under his chin, and kept his head up over the water. The little gray man was Saint Colman.

Colman Helps a Farmer

There was a man going home from Kinvara one night with a bag full of oats on the horse. But the bag fell on the ground, and though he strove to lift it again, he could not, for it was weighty. Then the saint himself, Saint Colman, came and helped him with it, and put it up again for him on the horse.

Colman Shows Respect for Respect

There was another man living up beyond Corcomruadh, and he never missed going to the blessed well that is above Oughtmana on the name day of the Saint. And at last it happened he was sick in his

bed and he could not go. So Saint Colman came to
the side of his bed and said, "It is often you came to
me, and now it is I myself am come to you."

4
The Wonders Told by the Ever-New Tongue

In the old times, the people used to look at the moon and at the sun and the rest of the stars, traveling and ever-traveling, and they watched the flowing and ever-flowing of the world's wells and rivers. They saw the joy and the sadness of the earth: the trance and the sleep that came over it with the coming of winter, and the rising of the world again with the coming of the summer.

But the people were like those who have their heads in bags or like those living in a dark house, for they did not understand the why and the what of these things. But then Philip the Apostle told the whole story of the making of heaven and earth at a great gathering in the east of the world.

This is the way that gathering was: it lasted through the four seasons under nine hundred white golden-crowned canopies upon the hill of Zion. And five thousand nine hundred and fifty tower-candles and precious stones were kindled there, giving out light that there might be no hindrance from any sort of weather.

Late now upon Easter Eve, the people gathered there heard a clear voice speaking the language of the angels, and the sound of it was like the laughter of an army or like the outcry of a very big wind— and yet it was no louder than the talk of friend in the ear of friend, and it was sweeter than any music. This was the voice of Philip the Apostle, for he had been sent out to tell the story of the making of the world. It is long he was speaking and these are some of the wonders that he told.

The Beginning and the Shape of the World

"In the beginning before all else, God was and is and will be, the High-King of the world, mightier than any king, mightier than any power, fiercer than any dragon, gentler than any child, brighter than the suns of heaven, holier than any saint, more loving than any mother. The shape of the visible world is known only to God, for all has been obscure to us who are of Adam's blood."

And when the sages heard the voice of Philip the Apostle, they asked him, "Who are you? Let us know your name and your substance and your appearance."

And Philip, the one who spoke with the ever-new tongue, said, "I was born of man and woman, and Philip was the name they gave me. The Lord God sent me to all the world to preach to them. Nine times has my tongue been cut from my head, and nine times have I continued to preach again. Wherefore, the household of heaven calls me the Ever-New Tongue."

The sages asked him, "What language do you speak to us?"

He said, "I speak with the speech of angels, with the language of the ranks of heaven. But the beasts of the sea and the reptiles, and all those who walk on four legs, and the birds, the snakes, and the creeping things, and even all the demons—they know this language. It is the language all shall speak at the End of Time."

And then he said, "I will tell you of the earth, and the making of the heaven and earth, and the formation of the world. All this happened because of Christ's Resurrection from the dead. For every material thing we see and touch, every element, every thing which we see in the world round about, all of it are combined in the Body in which Christ arose—and by that I mean the body of every human being, for in each and each is the Resurrection of the Body of Christ."

And then he said, "Human and earth are one. In the first place, see the wind and air, and consider the breath in the bodies of all who live. Next, think on the world's heat and fire and the boiling of water; this is the same that makes the red heat of our blood within our bodies. Then there is the matter of the sun and the other stars of heaven, and these are the glory and the light that shines from the eyes of human beings. Think next on the sea's bitterness and saltness; it is the same that makes the saltness of tears, the gall of the liver, and the wrath within our hearts. Then there is the matter of stones and the clay of the earth; this is the same as the mingling of flesh and bone in human beings, for we come from the same earth. But there are also flowers on the earth, of many colors and many shapes, and so too there are variations in the skin of our faces and the color of our cheeks."

He continued on, saying, "When Christ arose, all the world arose with him, for all the elements dwelled in the Body of Jesus. For unless the Lord had been Adam, and unless he had risen from death, the whole world would be destroyed on the day of Doom, and no creature of sea or land would be reborn. There would be neither earth nor kindred alive nor dead in all the world, had not the Lord ransomed them from before the foundation of the world. All would have perished thus without the renewal of the Resurrection."

The sages asked him, "If nothing without Christ hitherto existed, what was there before the day of Creation?"

And the Ever-New Tongue answered, "Every creature was with God, without beginning, without end, without sorrow or age or decay. There was no hour nor space where God existed not. He is not older or younger now than before. He thought, but there was no beginning to His thought, and so all the world has ever existed, because it exists only in God's thought."

Then the sages asked him, "Tell us now how the universe is arranged? What is its shape?"

Philip, the Ever-New Tongue, answered, "Every thing in all the world was created in roundness, though you may not see it. The heavens were made in circularity, and the seas, and the roundness of the earth. In roundness and circularity the stars travel the wheel of the universe, and souls too are round when they issue from their bodies. The high vault of heaven is round, and round is the orbit of sun and moon. Why is this? Because it tells us the shape of the Lord, who too is like a circle, without beginning or end, who has ever been, who ever will be, who made all things from forever. Therefore the world is embodied in a round shape."

The sages asked him then, "What was the material within all this roundness of heaven and earth?"

And he answered, "In the circuit of the universe is the material of the universe: cold and heat, light and dark, heavy and weightless, wet and dry, high and low, bitter and mild, strength and weakness, roaring sea and clouds of thunder, the scent of flowers and pillars of fire, and even the chant of angels. All these were in the round cloud, the multiform cloud from which came all the material of the universe, and is there that the stuff of hell was produced as well. If the angels who had sinned had remained true to the nature to which they were created, in the angelic radiance to which they were called, the material of heaven would have been as beautiful and bright as the kingdom of the holy angels."

The Seven Heavens

"As to the Seven Heavens that are around the earth," he told them next, "the first of them is the bright cloudy heaven that is the nearest and through which shines the moon. Beyond that are two flaming heavens; angels are in them that put fruitfulness in the clouds and in the sea, and beyond those is an ice-cold heaven, bluer than any blue, seven times colder than any snow, and out of that comes the shining of the sun. Two heavens there are above that again, bright like flame, and out of them shine the fiery stars. A high heaven, high and fiery, is above all the rest; highest of all it is, having within it the music of all that has been created and choirs of angels. In the belts of the seven heavens are hidden the twelve shaking beasts that have fiery heads upon their heavenly bodies, that are blowing twelve winds about the world. In the same belts are sleeping the dragons with fiery breath, tower-headed, blemished, that give out the crash of the thunders and blow lightnings out of their eyes."

The Secrets of the Sea

"The sea has three waters," he continued. "The first of them is a seven-shaped sea under the belly of the world. The second is a sea green and bright round about the earth on every side; ebbing and flood, it casts up its fruits. The third sea is a sea aflame, and nine winds are let out of the heavens to call it from its sleep; three score and ten and four hundred songs are sung, and it awakens. A noise of thunder comes roaring out of its wave-voice; flooding and ever flooding it is from the beginning of the world until God calls for the Sunday of all Creation. This sea is asleep until the thunders of the winds are awakened by the coming of God's Sunday from heaven, and by the music of the angels.

"Along with those great seas, there are many kinds of seas around the earth on all its flanks: a red sea having many precious stones, bright as the Flood, well colored, golden, between the lands of Egypt and the lands of India; sea bright, many-sanded, of the color of snow, in the north around the islands that lie there (so great is the strength of its waves that they break and scatter to the height of the clouds); then a sea that is waveless, black as a beetle, which no ship has escaped from it again that reached it except one boat only (by the lightness of its going and the strength of its sails), and shoals of beasts are lying in that sea; a sea is in the ocean to the south of the island of Ebian. At the first of the summer it rises in flood till it ebbs at the coming of winter; half the year it is in flood it is, and half the year always ebbing. Its beasts and its monsters mourn at the time of its ebbing and they fall into sadness and sleep. They awake and welcome its flooding, and the wells and the streams of the world increase; going and coming again they are through its valleys."

The Four Trees That Have a Life Like the Angels

Then he said, "The trees of the earth all come from the seeds of four trees that were planted by the High King of Heaven.

"First is one that bears its fruit three times every year. Bright green its first fruit is, and red the next, and the last is shining. When the first of the fruit is ripe, another grows out of its flowers, and every witless person tasting that fruit comes back into a right mind. No leaf has ever fallen from that tree, and there is no person having sickness or blemish that is not healed through coming under its shadow.

"Next is the Tree of Life in Paradise. No mouth that has tasted its fruit ever died. Twelve times it bears fruit every year, in every month a well-colored harvest; and the sweet smell of Paradise reaches out from it as far as a seven summer days' journey.

"Third is a tree that is shaped in the form of a human. Its blossoms quell every disease and every poison, and the sweet smell of its flowers is felt to the length of a journey of six summer days; precious stones are the kernels of its fruit. It banishes anger and envy from every heart that its juice has run over.

"Fourth is a tree that was never found by any human from the beginning of the world, except on the one day only when there was need of a tree for Christ's hanging. From its branches the Cross was made through which the world was saved. Seven times it bears fruit in the year, and seven times it changes its flowers, and the brightness of the moon and of the sun and the shining of the stars shine out of the flowers. Its leaves and its flowers sing together, and they have done so since the beginning of the world, two and seventy kinds of music at the coming of the winds. Three score birds and five and three hundred, bright like snow, golden-winged, sing many songs from its branches. They sing a true language together, but human ears do not recognize it, though it never ceases, and its sound is everywhere across the earth."

The Journey of the Sun

"God made on the fourth day the wandering stars of heaven," he said next, "and the fiery course of the sun that warms the world with the sense and the splendor of angels. The fiery sea laughs against the sun's journey; ranks of angels come together, welcoming his visit after the brightness of the night. He shines upon all.

"The first place he brightens is the stream beyond the sea, with news of the eastern waters. Then he lightens the ocean of fire and the seas of sulphur-fire that are round about the red countries. Next he shines upon the troops of boys in the pleasant fields, who send out their cry to heaven through dread of the beast that kills thousands of armies under the waves of the south. He shines then upon the mountains that have streams of fire, on the hosts that protect them in the plains. Then the ribs of the great beast shine, and the four and twenty champions rise up in the valley of pain. He shines over against the terrible many-thronged fence in the north that has closed around the people of hell. He shines on the dark valleys having sorrowful streams over their faces. He brightens the ribs of the beast that sends out the many seas around the earth, that sucks in again the many seas till the sands on every side are dry. He shines upon the many beasts that sleep their sleep of tears in the valley of flowers from the first beginning of the world; and on the sorrowful tearful plain, with the dragons that were set under the mist. He shines then upon the bird-flocks singing their many tunes in the flower-valleys; upon the shining plains with the wine-flowers that lighten the valley; he shines at the last on Adam's Paradise till he rises up in the morning from the east. There would be many stories now for the sun to tell about his journey, if he had but a tongue to give them out, but he only shines on and shines on."

The Nature of the Stars

"The stars now differ in their nature from one another," said the Ever-New Tongue. "Some are trembling with fiery manes over their faces. Others are like great dragons that blow light out from their mouths. Others run and then sleep until they are awakened by the shout of angels and the voices of dragons. Others run the same course again and again, with many kinds of music. They fall asleep when God's Sunday falls over the heavens, and then they awake and follow the same round."

The High and Ever-Living Birds

Next, the Ever-New Tongue told of the ever-living birds. "These birds give a welcome to the heat and to the colors of the summer; at midnight they awake and sing the sweet string-music; there never was seen upon the floor of the world any color that is not upon their wings.

"The wings of other birds shine in the nighttime like candles of fire; sickness is turned to health under the shadow of their wings. They fall into sleep and darkness in the cold time of the winter. They sing in their sleep a high pleasant song that is like the thunder of wind. At the first of the summer they awake.

"The birds in the islands between the east of Africa and the sky have feathers that have lasted from the very beginning of the world. Not one bird is missing, and there is no increase of their numbers. The sweet smell of the flowers, the taste of the seven wine-rivers of the plain where they have their dwelling: that is their lasting food. They sing their song with truth, till the coming of the song of the angels in the night.

"The three bird-flocks are divided, and each gives their share of music to the humming of the angels overhead. Swift as riders on horses they travel quickly through the air. Two birds and seventy and seventy thousand—this is no lie. This is the number in every flock of the birds.

"The birds sing a sweetness that tells the whole of the wonderful courses that God made before the world. They are well-wishers and the hope-bringers that tell out at the end of the nighttime all the wonders God will do. If we heard the music of these birds but once, we would long to hear it again until the day we died."

The Valley of Pain

Now, the Ever-New Tongue told of the Valley of Pain. "So great is the greatness of the cold there, that if a breath the like of it could be thrown into the world through the hole of a pipe, every bird in the air and every beast under the sea and everything living on the earth would die. So great is the fierceness of the fire there, that if some of it should be cast into the world through a pipe, all the waters would die before it, and the living beasts in the sea would burn. So great is the greatness of the hunger and thirst there, that if a share of it could be thrown into the world for one hour only, all beasts and people and of birds would perish in that hour through hunger and through thirst. So great is the greatness of the fear there, that if one grain of such fear should come into the world, all the creatures of the sea and of the air and the earth would fall into madness and lose their wits through the dint of the terror, and then they would die. Such is the greatness of the grief and the sorrow there, that if any of it could be cast through a pipe into the world, there would be no warmth, nor pleasure, nor faces of friends, nor wine, nor welcome, but every heart it came to would die from crying and grief."

The Hour of the Lord

"At midnight, the Lord arose and created the world," said he. "At midnight was made the circle that is the material of the world. At midnight Adam was shaped from the earth. At midnight a troop of angels scattered mortality over the earth. At midnight the Savior of the World was born at Bethlehem, and at midnight he was crucified and great darkness came over the world that lasted into the afternoon. At midnight the Lord did harry hell and loosed all souls who had been bound by the Enemy, the Destroyer of the Elements, the Robber and the Thief, the Old Plunderer who seeks to steal and spoil all that is. And at midnight the Lord did rise from the dead, and no one can describe His power and dignity and all He has done to serve the world from its beginning until its end."

The Form of the Lord

"Such is the beauty and brightness of the Lord's form," said he, "that whenever it is manifested, no hells can exist, for they are turned into radiance with the luster of Heaven, and they are the celestial Kingdom. If the hue and brilliance of the Lord was to shine forth on any soul, that one would know its loss as the deepest hell. All the souls to whom God has granted their desire to death-step into hell suffer torment because they have turned their faces away from the form of the Lord.

"But those whose death-step leads to the Lord's Kingdom hear sweet melodies. All the faces there turn to them with welcome, and the hosts have splendor and flaminess. This is the place of which the Lord said, 'Come, possess the Kingdom that has been prepared for you since the beginning of the world.' Here there will be health and great peace and love that cannot be defeated. No old age will be here. Delight will be given, and feelings will be clear as water. This a paradise sweet and abundant, filled with the splendor of angels, the brightness of justice, the meeting of the saints, and everlasting happiness. Good is never absent from this place, nor will it ever be. No one will suffer poverty, nor nakedness, nor hunger, nor thirst. Desire for that which is not will disappear from all hearts, and they will be at the great banquet for ever and ever with the Father, the Son, and the Holy Ghost, and all the saints. *Saecula saeculorum*, lifetime upon lifetime, world without end."

And this was but some of what Philip the Apostle told of the perfect, all-golden very God.

5
Other Saints
and Our Lord

The time Saint Mochaemhog made his dwelling-
place at Liath Mor, the King of Munster took a liking to the saint's meadow and put his horses into it.
When Mochaemhog got word of that, he went and
turned the horses out of the meadow.

The Cloud of Witnesses

The King was greatly angered then, and he gave
orders that he saint should be banished from the
country. But when Mochaemhog heard that, he went
straight to Cashel of the Kings, and he himself argued
with the King of Munster. That night, the King had a
vision: an old man, very comely and shining, came

to him and took him by the hand, and led him from the room to the southern wall of Cashel. From there, he saw the whole of Magh Femen filled with a host of white saints having the appearance of flowers. He asked what great host that was, and the old man said they were Blessed Patrick and the saints of Ireland that had come to the help of Mochaemhog.

Next, the old man took the King by the hand again and led him to the northern wall. And from there King saw the whole of Magh Mossaid filled with a shining flowery host. And the old man told him that was the host of Saint Brigit and all the holy women who had lived, brought there by Blessed Ita, who was the kindred of Mochaemhog and his fosterer.

And the next day the King disputed no more with Mochaemhog but said, "Since you have such a cloud of witnesses to attend you, I must give way."

Blessed Cellach's Lament

When Cellach, a saint of Connacht and a son of the king, was taken by his enemies, they put him in a hollow of an oak tree for the night. As he was wait-ing for his death, he sang these words:

> *My blessing to the morning*
> *that is as white as a flame;*
> *my blessing to Him that sends it,*
> *the brave new morning;*
> *my blessing to you, white proud morning,*
> *sister to the bright sun,*
> *morning that lights up my little book for me.*
> *It is you who are the guest in every house;*
> *it is you who shine on every race and every family;*
> *white-necked morning, gold-clear, wonderful.*

> *Carrion crow, grey-cloaked, sharp beaked;*
> *it is well I know your desire;*
> *you are no friend to Cellach!*

> *Och, raven, do your croaking;*
> *if you have hunger,*
> *do not leave this place*
> *till you get your fill of my flesh!*

The kite of the Yew Tree of Cluan Eo,
he will be rough in the struggle;
he will take the full of me with his grey claws;
it is not in kindness he will part from me!

But the great Son of Mary
is saying over my head,
"You will have earth, you will have Heaven;
there is a welcome before you, Cellach!"

The Wolf's Prophecy

It chanced one day not long after the coming of the Gauls from England into Ireland, there was a priest making his way through a wood of Meath. A man came to him and bade him for the love of God to come with him to confess his wife who was lying sick near that place. So the priest turned with him, and it was not long before he heard groaning and complaining that he thought was coming from a woman.

But when he came closer, it was a wolf he saw before him on the ground. The priest was afeared when he saw that and he turned away, but the man and the wolf spoke with him and bade him not to be afeared but to turn back to hear her confession. Then the priest took heart and sat down beside her.

And the wolf spoke to him and made her confession, and he anointed her. And when they were done, the priest began to think in himself that if she had such a mis-likeness upon her and yet had grace to speak, she might likely have grace and the gift of knowledge in other things, so he asked her about the strangers who were come into Ireland, and how things would go with. And the wolf said that the Gaul that had come into the country would put Ireland in bondage, until such time that the people of Ireland could free themselves.

Liban the Sea Woman

The time Angus Og sent away Eochaid and Ribh from the plain of Bregia that was his playing ground, he gave them the loan of a very big horse to carry all they had northward. Eochaid went on with the horse till he came to the Grey Thornbush in Ulster; and a well broke out where he stopped, and he made his dwelling-house beside it. He made a cover for the well and put a woman to mind it.

But one time she did not shut down the cover, and the water rose up and covered the Grey Thorn-bush, and Eochaid was drowned with his children; and the water spread out into a great lake that has the name of Loch Neach to this day. But Liban who was one of Eochaid's daughters was not drowned. She was in her sunny-house under the lake with her little dog with her for a full year, and God protected her from the waters.

And one day she said, "O Lord, it would be well to be in the shape of a salmon, to be going through the sea the way they do." Then one half of her took the shape of a salmon and the other half kept the shape of a woman; and she went swimming in the sea, with her little dog following her in the shape of an otter, never leaving her or parting from her at all.

One time Caoilte was hunting near Beinn Boirche with the King of Ulster, and they came to the shore of the sea. And when they looked out over it, they saw a young girl on the waves, and she swimming with

the side-stroke and the foot-stroke. And when she
came opposite them, she sat up on a wave, as anyone
would sit upon a stone or a hillock, and she lifted her
head and said, "Is not that Caoilte Son of Ronan?"

"It is myself surely," said he.

"It is many a day," she said, "since we saw you
upon that rock, and the best man of Ireland or of
Scotland with you, that was Finn son of Cumhal."

"Who are you, girl?" said Caoilte.

"I am Liban daughter of Eochaid, and I am in the
water these hundred years. I never showed my face
to anyone since the going away of the King of the
Fianna to this day. And what led me to lift my head
today," she said, "was to see yourself, Caoilte."

Just then the deer that were running before
the hounds made for the sea and swam out into it.
"Throw your spear to me, Caoilte!" said Liban.

Then he put the spear into her hand, and she
killed the deer with it, and sent them back to him
where he was with the King of Ulster. She threw him
back the spear, and with that she went away.

And that is the way she was until the time Beoan
son of Innle was sent by Comgall to Rome, to have

talk with Gregory and to bring back rules and orders. And when he and his people were going over the sea, they heard what was like the singing of angels under the currach.

"What is that song?" said Beoan.

"It is I myself am making it," said Liban.

"Who are you?" said Beoan.

"I am Liban daughter of Eochaid son Mairid, and I am going through the sea these three hundred years." Then she told him all her story, and how she had her dwelling-place under the ships' round hulls, and the waves were the roofing of her house, and the strands its walls. "And I am come now," she said, "to tell you that I will come to meet you on this day twelve-month at Inver Ollorba. Do not fail to meet me there for the sake of all the saints of Dalaradia."

And at the year's end, the nets were spread along the coast where she said she would come, and in the net of Fergus from Miluic she was taken. The clerks gave her her choice either to be baptized and go then and there to heaven, or to stay living through another three hundred years and at the end of that time to go to heaven. The choice she made was to die.

Then Comgall baptized her and the name he gave her was Muirgheis, the Birth of the Sea. So she died, and the messengers that came to carry her to her burying place were horned deer that were sent by the angels of God.

The Priesc and the Bees

There was a good honorable well-born priest, God's darling he was, a man holding to the yoke of Christ, and it happened he went one day to attend a sick man. As he was going, a swarm of bees came toward him, and he having the Blessed Body of Christ with him there.

When he saw the swarm, he laid the Blessed Body on the ground and with great love gathered the swarm into his bosom. Then he went on his way upon his journey, forgetting the Blessed Body where he had laid it.

After a while, the bees left him and went back and found the Blessed Body. They carried it away between them to their own dwelling place, where they gave kind honor to it and made a good chapel of wax for it, and an altar and a chalice and a pair of priests, shaping each out of wax with care, to stand before Christ's Body.

As for the priest, when he remembered that he had left Christ's Body, he went looking for it carefully, penitently, but he could not find it in any place. Laden with guilt, he went to confession, and he fretted through the length of a year as though beneath a great weight.

At the end of the year, an angel came to him and told him the way the Body of Christ was sheltered and honored. The angel bade him to bring all the people to see that wonder. They went there, and when they saw it, a great many of them believed, for God had not minded the priest's carelessness, nor seen it as a transgression, but had used it as occasion for His creatures to praise Him yet more.

Tuan, Son of Cairell

Finnen of Magh Bile, saint of the Gael, went once to Ulster to visit a rich fighting-man that had no good belief. He would not let Finnen or his people into his house, but left them fasting through the Sunday.

Then a very old clerk bade them to come with him. "Come to my dwelling-place," he said, "for it will be more fitting for you."

They went with him then, and passed the Lord's day with psalms and with preachings and with offerings. Then Finnen asked the old man his name.

"I am one of the men of Ulster," he said, "and I am now Tuan, son of Cairell. But I was once Tuan, grandson of Sera, son of Partholon's brother."

Then Finnen bade him tell all that had happened in Ireland from the time of Partholon, also called Bartholomew, and they said they would not eat with him until he had told them the stories of Ireland.

"It is hard not to be thinking of the word of God you have been giving out to us," said Tuan, "rather than any story I have to tell."

But Finnen said, "You have leave to tell us now your own story, and the story of Ireland."

"Five times," Tuan said then, "Ireland has been taken since the Flood. Three hundred years after the Flood, Partholon and his people took it, bringing with them farming and cooking and brewing and building. Then, in the space between two Sundays, a sickness came upon them, so that they all died but one man only. I myself am that one," he said.

"After that I was going from hill to hill and from cliff to cliff, keeping myself from wolves through two and twenty years, and all Ireland was empty. Then the withering of age came upon me, and I was in waste places and my legs failed me, and I took to hiding in caves. Then Nemed, my father's brother, came into Ireland with his people, and I saw them from the cliffs, but I avoided them, for I was hairy, clawed, withered, grey, naked, sorrowful, miserable," he said.

"But one night in my sleep I saw myself going into the shape of a stag, and I was truly in that shape, young and glad in my mind. There grew upon my head two antlers having three score points, and I was the leader of the herds of Ireland, and there was a great herd of stags about me whatever way I went. That is the way I spent my life through the time of Nemed and his race, but they all died in the end. Then the withering of age came upon me again, and I went away from both men and wolves. One time I was at the door of my cave, I remember it yet, and

I knew I was yet once more going from one shape into another," he said.

"This time into the shape of a wild boar I went, and I was in that shape truly. I was young and glad in my mind, and I was the king of the boar-herds of Ireland, and I went the round of my dwelling until I returned to Ulster, where I once more took on the shape of a man," he said.

"Then Semion son of Stariath and his people took this island. After them were the Fir Domnann and the Firbolg and the Galliana, and all these lived their time in Ireland. And age came upon me, and my mind was troubled. I could not do the things I was used to do. I went back to my own place, and I remembered every shape I was in before. I fasted my three days as I had always done, and then I had no strength left. After that, I went into the shape of a great hawk and my mind was glad again. I was able to do everything. I said to myself that dearer to me each day was God, the Friend who had shaped me," he said.

"Then Beothach son of Iarbonel the prophet took this island from the people who were in it. And then came the Tuatha De Danaan and the An-De. Where they came from the learned do not know, but it seems likely they came from heaven, because of their skill and the excellence of their knowledge," he said.

"I was a long time in the shape of that hawk till I outlived all the races that had taken the land of Ireland. Then the sons of Miled took the island by force from the Tuatha De Danaan. I was in the shape of the hawk yet, in the hollow of a tree by a river. My mind was sorrowful, and all the birds came to me quietly. There I fasted three days and three nights until sleep fell upon me. When I awoke, I had gone into the shape of a salmon. God put me into the river and I was in it," he said.

"It is well content I was then, strong and well nourished, and my swimming was good. I escaped from every net and every danger, from the claws of hawks and from the hands of fishermen and their spears, though their marks are on me yet. And when God, my ever-help, thought it time, because the beasts were following me and I was known to every fisherman in every pool, the fisherman of Cairell, king of that country, took me and brought me to the queen, I remember it well," he said.

"The man put me on a spit and roasted me, and then served me to the queen, who had a desire for fish. She ate me, and I went into her womb. I remember well the time I was in her womb and what each one said to her in the house, and all that was done in Ireland through that time. I remember after my birth when speech came to me as it comes to every person, and I knew all that was going on in Ireland. I was a seer, and they gave me the name of Tuan son of Cairell. After that, Patrick came with the faith to Ireland, and I was baptized and believed in the Only-King of all things and of the Elements."

After Tuan had told all that, Finnen and his people stayed there through a week talking with him. And every history and every genealogy that is in Ireland, comes from him—or if not from him, then from Fintain, who Tuan said was older even than himself, since he was son of Bochra, son of Bith, son of Noah. For it is by these stories that we know the world.

How Conchubar the High King Died for Christ

When Conchubar High King of Ireland was fighting in Connacht, he was wounded in the head by a hard ball that lodged there. Then Fintain the great healer tended him, and took a thread of gold that was the same color as the King's hair and sewed up the wound. Fintain bade the king to be careful and not to give way to anger or to passion, and not to be running or riding on a horse.

So through seven years, Conchubar stayed in his quietness until the day of the Crucifixion. And on that day he noticed a change come over the world, and the sun darkened until the moon was shining. Conchubar asked his druid what was the meaning of this darkness.

"It is the Son of God," said the druid, "who is at this moment meeting His death."

"If he had called out to me," said Conchubar, "I would have gone to Him, a hardy fighter, my lips twitching, until the great courage of a champion broke the gap of battle. I would give my strength, my all to God's Son, with a wild shout, with the keening of a full lord, with full loss of all I hold dear. I would call upon the army of the heavenly ones, that their ready and beautiful help would relieve Him; beautiful the fight I would make for God's Son who is dying. I would not rest although my own body was broken. How can we not cry, when He is more worthy than any worthy king? I would go to death for His safety. It crushes my heart to know He is suffering."

And with that, he was overcome with passion, and he took his sword and rushed at an oakwood that was near at hand. From the greatness of the anger that gripped him, the wound in his head burst, and the ball struck his brain.

And that is the way Conchubar King of Ireland met with his death. And God counted it that he had given his life for Christ.

A Praise of Caillen and His Blessed Death

Caillen, saint of the Gael, was reared and taught by Finntain, the high elder of Ireland until his hundredth

year was at an end. Then Finntain sent Caillen to
the East so that he could bring back knowledge to
the folk of Ireland. Caillen stayed there in the East
through the length of two hundred years.

At last, an angel brought him back to Ireland, to
the Yew Tree at Baile's Strand, to live out the rest of
his life.

"And the reason I stay here," he said, "in Ireland
of many crosses, is that I never saw to this day a
country that is more blessed."

Caillen did many marvels, an unebbing sea of
wonders in lasting praise of his Master. Columcille
came and stayed with him a while at the place of
Baile's Yew Tree. His choice place it was of all he
had ever seen, north or east, south or west.

When God thought it time Caillen should go to
heaven, the people of heaven were standing up,
waiting for him. Caillen went in the church of Mochaemhog then, where the children of Lir had been
baptized, and he told a vision he had that night,

"And it vexed my heart and my head," he said,
"for I saw in it the Saxons coming across the sea,
and I saw Ireland in great bondage under them.

And it is time for me to go to heaven," he said, "for I have fulfilled five hundred years tonight. And when my body is buried," he said, "do not fear, for there will be a host of angels near me. For three hundred angels have always been around me at my rising and at my lying down in my bed; and I never said the Hours until I heard the people of Heaven joining in with me."

If the stars of the sky, and the sands of the sea, and the grass and the rest of the herbs of the earth, and the dew that is on them were all counted, it would not be enough to tell all the wonders done by blessed Caillen. Only an angel could do so.

The Calling of Martin the Miller

A miller Martin was, and the Blessed Mother and the Child came to him one time at his mill. The Mother held out a few grains of wheat in her hand and said, "Put those in the quern and turn the wheel for me."

"It is no use," said he, "to put in a little handful of grains like that."

"It is use," said the Blessed Mother.

So he put them in the quern then and turned the wheel, and there were ten sacks in the place all filled with the flour that came from those few grains. And when Saint Martin saw that, he sold the mill and all that he had, and he went following after the Blessed Mother and the Child.

Martin and the Grass-Corn

Martin went to a house one time, where the farmer who owned the house was out scattering water on the field, for there was red heat that year and no rain. The farmer had the seed sown, but he did not think the corn would grow unless he watered it.

The woman of the house told that to Martin while she was mixing dough. Martin asked for a bit of the dough, and she gave it, for he looked as though he were a poor man. Martin put the bit of dough she gave him in the oven and went on his way, leaving it there. And when the woman of the house opened the oven after a while, there was grass-corn growing up through the dough, and a drop of dew on the top of every blade. Martin did that to show the man of the house that God could make grass-corn grow even in the heat of the oven.

Marbhan's Hymn of Content

Marbhan, the brother of Guaire, King of Connacht, left his brother's house and his share of his father's inheritance, and went into a lonely wild place near to where Saint Colman settled.

King Guaire followed his brother there and asked him to come back where he could sleep on a bed and not be laying his head on a hard fir tree to sleep. But Marbhan would not leave the place he had chosen, for he said he was well content to be in a little cabin where no one knew where he was except God.

And he made a song of it:

The size of my cabin is small, not too small;
many are its lucky paths;
a beautiful woman, a blackbird,
sings a sweet strain upon the roof.

Goats and swine are lying down about it;
tame pigs, wild pigs, grazing deer
a badger's brood, foxes to meet them in peace,
and all that is delightful.

An apple tree is ready like an inn, lucky;
a thick little bush with fistfuls of hazel-nuts;
green, full of branches.

A rowan tree, a sloe bush;
dark black thorns, plenty of food;
acorns, haws, yew berries; bearberries, blackberries.

Buzzing of bees, the heifers lowing,
the cackle of wild geese before the winter;
the voice of the wind against the branches;
that is delightful music.

"In the eyes of Christ," he told his brother, "I am no worse off than yourself, Guaire. And there is not one hour of fighting or the noise of quarrels in my house."

And when Guaire heard that, he said he would be willing to give up his inheritance and his kingship to be in the company of Marbhan.

Guaire's Kindness to the Bush

One time there was a great troop of poets in Guaire's house in the wintertime, and a woman of the poets' household had a desire for ripe blackberries. But everybody said there were no blackberries to be got, ripe or unripe, at that time of the year.

But as one of Guaire's people was out in the fields, he saw a bush that was covered with a cloak, and under the cloak the blackberries were ripe and sound. The man brought them to the woman, and she was happy, but all wondered how the bush came to be covered.

This was the way that happened: King Guaire was going through the field at harvest time, when the thorns of the bush took hold of the cloak he was wearing and held it. Guaire was not willing to refuse so much as a bush that asked anything of him, and he left the cloak there on the branches.

Mochae and the Bird

On the Island of One Ridge on Loch Cuan Mochae the Beautiful, saint of the Gael, built his church and the dwelling of the brothers. He went out, now, one day, and seven score young men with him, cutting rods to build the church, and he himself was working like the rest of them.

He sat down beside his load to rest a moment, and just then he heard a bird singing on the branch of a blackthorn that was close at hand. It was more beautiful than any of the birds of the world, and it said, "This is hard work you are doing, Clerk."

"It is what is required of me to build a church of God," said Mochae. "But who is it speaking to me?"

"An angel of God is here," said the bird, "one of the people of Heaven."

"A welcome to you. But why have you come?"

"To speak the word of God and to cheer you for a while."

"That pleases me well," said Mochae.

Then the little bird from Heaven sang to Mochae three songs from the tree where he was, and fifty years were in each song of those songs. Mochae stayed there listening to it through three times fifty years, in the middle of the wood with his bundle of rods by his side. They did not wither, and the time seemed to him as if it was but one hour of the day.

Then the angel left him, and Mochae went back to the church with his load. He found there a house of prayer that had been built to his memory by his friends, and he wondered at seeing a church built there. When he came to the house where the brothers were, there was no one in it that knew him. But when he told his story and the way the bird had sung to him, they all knelt before him and made a shrine with the rods he had carried. And after that they built a church on the spot where he had listened to the bird, and the walls of that church are standing yet.

The Mad Priest

A madness came upon a man of God, and he stripped off every bit of clothing. Out and away he ran through the country, bare naked, carrying on his head a very large book he himself had written. He grew calmer after that, but nothing anyone could do would bring him back into the house of his father, and he ate only the plants of the earth.

His father was a miller, and every night the mad son lay down in the mill with the big book under his head for a pillow. Daytimes he spent in a wide field where there was a great flock of sheep and of lambs. He would sit down in the middle on a stone, and the sheep and lambs would gather around him, and he read to them from his book until his voice grew tired. Then each lamb and sheep would come to him and lick his hands.

Once a woman came by, without him knowing, and she heard him giving a sermon to the sheep. "Listen to me," he was saying to them, "you who are without sin. You are under the care of God, and there is grass growing for you and herbs, and there are nice white dresses upon you to keep you dry and warm; and there is no Judgment upon you after your death, and you are happier by far than the children of Eve." And he told them of the coming of the Son of God to the earth, and the bad treatment and the abuse that He was given, and a great many other things he told them out of the book.

One night late, his father grew uneasy about him, and he got a lantern and went to the mill, taking another man along with him. When they opened the door, they saw the whole mill lit up as bright as if it were the sun was lighting it. And the mad priest was lying there in his sleep, the big book under his head, and a great shining ram stood on each side of him, guarding him.

The Day of Our Death

At the time of death, the soul is tired and the body takes its rest. But a shadow goes from the person and wanders, back to the place most called home, and there she does what must be done to prepare her for Heaven. Then the angels who have been her special friends all through her life come out to greet her.

And when we reach Heaven, we are each thirty-three years old, just in our bloom. And in that lasting bloom, we will work for those who still live in the world, doing them good. We will live in the hidden houses that lie beyond the visible world, talking with the angels and the saints, and we will protect those on earth and wake them at their deaths.

Our Lord

As to our Lord, He is no stranger to the land of the Celts. He walks the whole of the land without shoes and barefoot, and now the lamb is always innocent because of Our Lord. The robin also keeps Our Lord's memory, for he wears a bit of the blood from the Cross, and he sings a friendly song to us.

Now we no longer see the Lord, not often, but be sure He is in every place. He sits and listens while people talk, His hand on His knee, His head turned to whoever is speaking, listening and listening. And when someone needs help, He puts him right. Our Lord does not go to bed, but keeps watch all through the night. And so we should trust Him, for as He did guard the saints of old, still He guards us today.

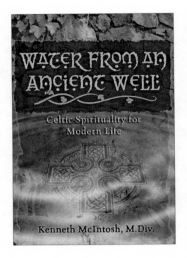

**Water from
an Ancient Well:
Celtic Spirituality
for Modern Life**
Author: Kenneth McIntosh,
M.Div.
Price: $24.95
Paperback
E-book Available
352 pages
ISBN: 978-1-933630-98-4

Discover the world of the ancient Celtic Christians and find practical insights for living in the twenty-first century.

"When I was reading *Water from an Ancient Well*, I sometimes felt like I taking a spiritual pilgrimage to Cano Cristales, the most beautiful river in the world or the river of five colors. Located near the town of La Macarena in Colombia, South America, the river is famous for its colorful blotches of blue, green, black, and red causing some to call it the river that ran away to paradise. If you want to run away to paradise for a couple of days, and drink living water from a source unlike any other, read Kenneth McIntosh's deeply satisfying book."

—**Leonard Sweet**, best-selling author and professor.

Earth Afire with God: Celtic Prayers for Ordinary Life

Author: Anamchara Books
Price: $12.95
Paperback
E-book Available
120 pages
ISBN: 978-1-933630-96-0

Here are prayers and blessings to sanctify your daily life. They will remind you to look for the holiness of the everyday; they will show you the real presence of God in Creation. Illumine your life with the ancient Celts' perspective on prayer. Each glimpse we have of the Earth's beauty, each ordinary sound we hear, every bite of food we eat, and even our daily routines, can all reveal God.

Kenneth McIntosh, author of *Water from an Ancient Well, Celtic Spirituality for Modern Life*, writes, "This book knocks the dust off ancient treasures—such as selections from the *Carmina Gadelica*—and also introduces some lovely new prayers, all written from the Celtic perspective."

**Brigid's Mantle:
A Celtic Dialogue
Between Pagan
and Christian**
Author: Lilly Weichberger
and Kenneth McIntosh
Price: $14.95
Paperback
E-book Available
ISBN: 978-1-62524-262-4

Long ago, the story goes, Brigid flung out her mantle over the world. Beneath its shelter, the Earth and its people could find healing, insight, and growth. This legend, shared by both Celtic Pagans and Celtic Christians, makes the point that a mantle is not a box, a small rigid container meant to keep some things inside while excluding others. Instead, a mantle is wide, flexible, inclusive. Using this as their central metaphor, the authors—one a Pagan healer and the other a Christian minister—engage in a dialogue that is ultimately about what it means to be spiritual, to be a person of faith. With Brigid, as both a Pagan Goddess and a Christian saint, at the center of their dialogue, the authors first provide the historical foundation for the Celtic culture, past and present. They build on this a concept of Celtic spirituality that embraces the arts, Nature, the supernatural world, compassion for those in need, and gender equality.

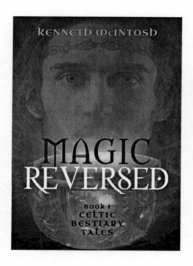

Magic Reversed
Author: Kenneth McIntosh
Price: $17.95
Paperback
E-book Available
ISBN: 978-1-62524-240-2

This book can be enjoyed on several levels. It's an action-packed young adult fantasy, brimming with adventure, danger, and romance. Young adult readers will relate to the tension between Finn and Freya that slowly blossoms into something deeper. Fantasy-lovers of all ages will be delighted to encounter characters from Celtic mythology: the wizard Merlin, the Goddess Brigid, and the ravenous walking dead spawned by the Dark Lord's cauldron. At the same time, those who are attracted to Celtic spirituality will find strands of symbolism, like gold threads in an ancient tapestry, meshed unobtrusively with this tale of a young hero's journey to save his world.

Anamchara Books

Books to Inspire
Your Spiritual Journey

In Celtic Christianity, an *anamchara* is a soul friend, a companion and mentor (often across the miles and the years) on the spiritual journey. Soul friendship entails a commitment to both accept and challenge, to reach across all divisions in a search for the wisdom and truth at the heart of our lives.

At Anamchara Books, we are committed to creating a community of soul friends by publishing books that lead us into deeper relationships with God, the Earth, and each other. These books connect us with the great mystics of the past, as well as with more modern spiritual thinkers. They are designed to build bridges, shaping an inclusive spirituality where we all can grow.

To find out more about Anamchara Books and order our books, visit **www.AnamcharaBooks.com** today.

Anamchara Books

Vestal, New York 13850
www.AnamcharaBooks.com

CPSIA information can be obtained
at www.ICGtesting.com
Printed in the USA
FSOW02n2155020715
8511FS